by
MOREY AMSTERDAM

with drawings by Sheila Greenwald

The Citadel Press
New York

To KAY, my wife
who has a wonderful sense of humor,
obviously

contents

I would like my readers to know that I go swimming every day of the year . . . so even if you don't like the book, remember I'm clean.

MOREY AMSTERDAM

Keep
Laughing

chapter one

CHILDREN

(Or: "Shut your mouth and eat.")
(Or: "Out of the mouth of babes comes . . . oatmeal!")

Children aren't what they used to be. Today they're men and women: which teaches us that we should work hard, save our money and when we're old we'll be able to afford all the things that only kids enjoy.

I had a very happy childhood. I never remember my father hitting me, except in self-defense. My mother was a smart woman. Everytime I'd take the cod-liver oil, she'd give me a dime for my piggy bank . . . then when the piggy bank got full, she'd break it open and use the money to buy more cod-liver oil.

Kids today are no worse than they were twenty years ago. They just have better weapons. Actually a juvenile delinquent is a kid who does the same things you used to do, only he gets caught.

I went to a very tough school. We had the only class with a "look-out." We even celebrated Al Capone's birthday and got the Academy award for "spit-balls," but the teacher never chased after us . . . *we nailed her to the floor!* Yeah . . . kids do funny things . . . as to wit:

One blistering hot day when we had guests for dinner, my wife asked our little eight-year-old Cathy to say the blessing. Embarrassed she said, "But Mother, I don't know any."

"Oh, just say what you've heard me say," my wife told her.

Obediently she bowed her head and said, "Oh, Lord, why did I invite these people here on this hot day!"

In a department store one day, I saw a little boy screaming and kicking up an awful fuss. He kept yelling that he wanted a cap pistol. I asked him, "When you holler like that does it always get you what you want?" The little "devil" answered, "Well sometimes it does and sometimes it doesn't, but it's no trouble to holler!"

"Your face is clean, but how did you get your hands so dirty?"

"Washing my face."

One modern baby to another: "If I had my life to live over again, I'd be a bottle baby. I'm sick and tired of having cigarette ashes flicked in my face."

A small boy was looking through the hole in the fence around a nudist colony. "Hey," he said to his friend, "lotsa people in there." "Men or ladies?" his friend asked. "You can't tell," the boy replied. "They ain't got no clothes on."

"What's your favorite sea food?"
"Salt water taffy."

A teen-age boy sent his little girl friend the first corsage she had ever received. With it came this note: "With all my love and most of my allowance."

Two small boys were visiting in a museum. As they stood in front of a mummy with a sign under it that read "2533 B.C.", one of them said, "I wonder what that means?" The other said, "Oh, that's probably the license number of the car that hit him."

"Mama, can I go out and play?"
"What? With those holes in your socks?"
"No, with the kids across the street."

Then there was the teen-ager whose parents told him about the birds and bees . . . so . . . for six months he went steady with a sparrow.

Or . . . how about the schoolboy who always said that when he grew up, he was gonna be a pirate, and sure enough, today he is a TV repairman.

MOTHER: If you don't stop practicing on that saxophone, I'll go crazy.

KID: Too late, Ma. I stopped an hour ago!

Never slap a child in the face. Remember there is a place for everything.

The mother of five children looked tired and worn as she boarded the elevator. Two of the younger kids had ice-cream cones and one of them brushed up against a woman wearing a gorgeous mink stole. "For goodness sakes, watch yourself," yelled the tired mother. "You're getting fur all over your ice cream!"

"My father planted a tree right in the middle of our front-room."

"That's silly."

"I know it doesn't look good, but it keeps our dog off the street at nights."

An Indian chief called his tribe together and spoke thusly: "What little papoose push outhouse over cliff?"

There was no answer.

"Big Chief tell story. Long time ago, George Washington was a little boy. Him cut down cherry tree. His papa ask who did it and George say he do it. He no tell lie. He no get whipping. Now . . . who push outhouse over cliff?"

A little Indian boy raised his hand and admitted that he had done it, whereupon his father gave him a "hit-in-the-head" that sent him sprawling. The kid finally got up off the ground, looked at the Indian chief and said, "You say

George Washington no tell lie . . . no get whipping." The chief replied, "George Washington's father not in cherry tree when George cut it down."

Johnny's teacher wrote to his mother: "Johnny is a bright boy, but he seems to spend all his time thinking about girls."

Johnny's mother wrote to his teacher: "If you find a cure, let me know. I'm having the same trouble with his father."

Excerpt from composition by a fifth-grade boy: "When this bullfighter killed the bull, he cut him up and ate him. Then he started to sing. A hunter heard him singing and shot him. The moral of the story is: When you're full of bull, keep your mouth shut."

"My brother ran a hundred yards in six seconds."

"You're nuts. The world's record is more than nine seconds."

"My brother knows a short cut."

A teen-age girl came down the steps in her first evening gown. Her family watched her openmouthed, all except her seven-year-old brother, who said, "Aren't you gonna wear a shirt?"

Apropos of the above, two small boys were looking at a bunch of debutantes in their low-cut formals, when one boy said to the other: "I'm sure glad I ain't a girl. Lookit all the neck they gotta wash!"

"Jimmy, did you put fresh water in the goldfish bowl?"

"Naww . . . they didn't drink up what I gave 'em yesterday."

When my son Greg was five years old his teeth were in bad shape and the dentist recommended "no sweets." However, it was his birthday and what's a boy's birthday party without ice cream, cake and candy? Well, we decided to substitute Jello and placed a big shimmering mold of it in front of him. He just stared at the Jello and watched it shake. When we told him to go ahead and eat it, he said, "I can't. It ain't dead yet!"

My brother Mannie's little daughter Barbara had been a "naughty" girl and was sent to bed without her dinner. As her older sister Claudia was passing the bedroom door, she heard Barbara just finishing her prayers: "And God bless Mommy and Daddy, but don't send them any more children. They don't know how to treat the ones they've got now."

> Mule in the barnyard, lazy and sick,
> Boy with pin on the end of a stick,
> Boy gives jab,
> Mule gives kicks,
> Services tomorrow, half past six.

"What's the bump on your head?"

"It's from my tonsil operation."

"How could you get a bump on your head from your tonsil operation?"

"They ran out of ether."

When my daughter Cathy was four years old, she got a
pretty bad sunburn which soon started to peel. Standing
in front of the mirror watching little patches of dry skin
peel off, she said, "Here I am only four years old, and I'm
starting to wear out already."

A Scotch couple were discussing the approaching birthday of their small son. The mother asked, "What are we gonna get little Angus for his birthday, a bicycle, or a tricycle?" His father replied, "Why don't we wait till the wintertime and get him an icycle. . . . ?"

A small boy was busy raking the leaves on his front lawn. A neighbor asked him, "Is your father gonna give you something for doing that?" The boy answered, "He's gonna give me something if I don't."

Which reminds me. . . . When I was a small boy, I used to go on whaling expeditions with my father . . . out to the woodshed!

"Why did you kick your little brother in the stomach?"
"It was his fault, he turned around."

Once upon a time, there was a boy named Jack Beanstalk. His mother told him to take the cow to market and sell it since they needed the money. As they were crossing a railroad track, the train came along, hit the cow, and knocked his tail off. So, Jack had to sell the cow wholesale, because he couldn't *retail* it.

"Daddy, Daddy, Mommy just backed the car over my new bicycle."
"I told you not to leave it in the living room."

SONG TITLE: Twenty-five children has Mrs. O'Brien,
She feels fine, but the stork is dyin'!

My mother and father keep fighting,
They rant and they rave and they shout,
"Who is your father?" somebody asked,
"That's what they're fighting about."

A lady with nine children got on a bus. The bus driver
asked her, "Lady, are those all your kids or is this a picnic?"

She replied, "They're all mine, and believe me it's *no*
picnic!"

An old maid aunt asked her nephew if he would let her
kiss him, for a nickel. The kid said, "I get more than that
for taking castor oil."

PROUD MOTHER: Harold, it's nice to see you sitting there
so quietly, looking at your father, while he takes his nap.
FRESH KID: I'm watchin' his cigarette burn down to his
fingers.

I used to think when I was young
That girls were sweet as pie,
But when I think of what I thunk,
I think I thunk a lie!

"My brother was overcome by the heat."
"In this cool weather?"
"He fell in the furnace!"

"Mommy, I just knocked over the ladder in the garden."
"Go tell your father."
"He knows. He's hanging from the bedroom window."

One night we had a bunch of the fellows over to play Gin Rummy, so we put our little girl to bed about seven o'clock. At eleven o'clock that night, this poor little thing walks into the room in her nightie, soaking-wet, goes up to where the men are playing cards, and with an accusing finger, said, "You, you, or you left the seat up, *I fell in!*"

"Do you say your prayers before you eat?"
"Naww, my Ma is a good cook."

Never underestimate a child's knowledge of what goes on around him. A little boy asked his mother where he came from and she told him, *The Stork.* When he asked the same question about his parents and about his grandparents, she gave him the same answer, *The Stork.* "Whatdy'a know." said the kid, "there hasn't been any marital relations in our family for three generations."

Another boy asked his father the same question, but this father very quietly and in detail, told him all about "the birds and the bees." "So that's it," said the kid. "I figured that the stork had too short a wingspread to carry an eight to ten lb. load."

Many years ago, I was "going with" a girl who invited me to her home for dinner. All through the meal, their pet poodle kept nipping at my ankles. I was doing my best to make a good impression, so I tried to ignore it, but when the dog started getting to the "white meat," I said, "I don't like to complain, but your dog keeps biting at my leg." Her kid brother spoke up. "Pay no attention to him, Mister, he's just jealous. You're eating out of his plate."

My young niece, Claudia, complained she was at the "awkward age." Too old for Castoria and too young for Serutan.

"What does 'unselfish' mean?"
"It means to need something and not take it."
"I was unselfish this morning."
"Really?"
"Yep, I needed a bath and I didn't take it."

I was a boy scout till I was sixteen . . . then I became a *Girl Scout.*

"I'm gonna enter my dog in the dog show."
"Do you think he'll win anything?"
"No, but he'll meet some nice dogs."

Once upon a time, there was an explorer up near the North Pole, and he found a little Eskimo boy crying. He found out the little boy cried all the time, so he asked him why. "Why not?" said the kid, "if you ate nothing but whale meat all the time, you'd blubber too."

"Mommy can I go in swimming?"
"No, its too dangerous."
"Daddy's in swimming."
"He's insured."

A small boy asked his father for a half-dollar to go out and buy some ice cream and candy. His father, trying to point out the value of money, said, "When I was your age, I was lucky to get a nickel for candy." The boy smiled

23

patronizingly at his father and said, "Gee, I'll bet you're glad you're living with us now."

"My uncle has a gold medal for swimming, a silver cup for golfing, and a beautiful watch for pole vaulting."
"He must be a wonderful athlete."
"No, he runs a hock shop."

The teacher told the children in the class that she wanted them to write a composition that involved religion, history, and mystery. Some bright lad turned in this short one. *"Holy Moses, the Queen is pregnant. I wonder who did it?"*

"Do you have a family tree?"
"We ain't even got a flowerpot."

My girl and I went out to the park to pick flowers. Her kid brother came along, so we picked flowers.

One day, when I was a kid, I sat on the floor doing my homework. My father was seated in a chair nearby, reading the evening paper.
"Dad," I asked, "who discovered the Mississippi River?"
He replied, "I don't know."
"What year was gold found in California?" I asked.
Again he said he didn't know.
Then I asked him, "What year did Magellan circumnavigate the globe?"
Again he said, "I don't know."
Then I said, "Dad, you don't mind me asking all these

questions, do you?" And he replied, "Of course not, son . . . how else are you going to learn?"

Around the holidays, you'll notice that the only thing stronger than Mother's love is Father's breath!

My parents told me not to smoke. . . . I don't.
Nor listen to a naughty joke. . . . I don't.
They made it clear I mustn't wink at handsome guys,
Or even think about intoxicating drink. . . . I don't.
To flirt or dance is very wrong. . . . I don't.
Wild youth . . . chase boys . . . wine and song. . . . I don't.
Kiss no fellas . . . not even one. . . .
I don't even know how it's done. . . .
You wouldn't think I have much fun. . . .
I don't!

—Anonymous

"Before you eat that banana you're supposed to take off the peeling."
"What for? I know what's inside."

How to Tell the Correct Temperature for Baby's Bath: Put the baby in the bath water. If the kid turns red, it's too hot. If he turns blue, it's too cold. If the water turns black, the kid really needed a bath!

Two small boys were discussing their problems. "Gee," said one, "my mother won't even let me come in for dinner unless I wash up, change my shirt, and comb my hair." "Nothin' like that at my house," said the other kid, "My mother don't care how much dirt I make around the place, and I don't have to wash or nothin' before dinner." "Boy," said the first youngster, "I sure wish I had a dirty mother like you."

While a clergyman was preparing his sermon, his little daughter was watching him.

"Daddy," she asked, "does God tell you what to say?"

"Of course, child," the father answered, "why do you ask?"

"Then why," said the little girl, "do you keep scratching some of it out?"

My mother-in-law who is a devotee of that kind of "stuff" went to see a spiritualist medium. She took our little girl, Cathy, with her. At the time, Cathy was about five years old. After the spiritualist "brought back" the voice of Mom's departed uncle, little Cathy said, "I wanna talk to my grandpa." The spiritualist told her to sit quietly and concentrate. Soon an eerie voice came over what must have been a loud-speaker system and said, "Hello little Cathy, this is Grandpa." "Grandpa," she said, "what are you doing in Heaven? You ain't dead yet."

chapter two

LOVE AND MARRIAGE

(Or: Love is like hash . . . you have to have confidence
in it to enjoy it.)
(Or: Marriage is like a cafeteria. . . . You take what
looks good to you, and pay for it later.)
(Or: If a girl don't marry the guy she wants, I pity the
guy she gets.)

I've been married for seventeen years, and I'm still in love
with the same girl. If my wife ever finds out, she'll kill
me. I was just kidding. My wife is a doll. She's a little

27

effeminate, but very sweet. When we were "going to-gether," I gave her so many gifts I had to marry her for my money. Our wedding was a very formal affair, but very quiet. My father-in-law carried a white shot-gun with a Maxim silencer. My wife comes from a wonderful family. She doesn't exactly *come* from a wonderful family; she brought 'em along. Her father and mother live with us. I guess it's all right, though; it's their house. We spent our honeymoon at a lovely place in the mountains called "The Bedside Manor." "It's wonderful for rheumatism; all our guests get it." They had little signs over the bed reading, "Sleep here and the angels watch over you." A couple of 'em bit me! When we walked in, I signed the register and just as the ink was drying, a cockroach walked right over my name. Wasn't bad enough to find 'em in bed; they hadda come down to see what room we were in. I was busy signing the register, and my wife was busy "thumbing her nose" at the house detective. Novelty night! They gave us the Bridal Suite. Big deal, engaged nine years and they give us the Bridal Suite! Oh well, you can rent a ballroom; you don't have to dance. The next morning after our wedding night, my bride said to me, "Honey, I have a confession to make: I have asthma." I said, "Thank Heaven, I thought you were hissing me!" Which reminds me of a few thousand stories, such as:

A man walked into an insurance company and reported that his car had been stolen, and he wanted to get the money for a new car. The insurance adjuster told him, "We don't give you the money; we just replace your old car with a new one." "So," replied the man, "if that's the

28

way you do business, I'd like to cancel the policy on my wife."

"They're such a nice couple; too bad they're not good enough for each other."
"What makes you say that?"
"I've been talking to both families."

My wife meets me halfway on everything. It's my house, she lives in it; it's my car, she drives it; it's my money, she spends it. She's only waiting for one thing. She wants me to have a nervous breakdown so she can go to Florida.

POEM: My heart told me I needed a wife . . . my life was
       in a rut.
      My heart told me I needed a wife . . . I wish my
       heart would keep its big mouth shut!

MOTHER: Daughter, before you become engaged to that man, be sure he is kind and considerate.
DAUGHTER: Oh, I'm sure he is, Mother. Only the other day, he told me he put his shirt on a horse that was scratched. Isn't that nice?

Two friends of mine recently married. He had been married six times before, and she had been married five times before. You should have seen the wedding invitations. They read: *Be sure and show up. This is no amateur affair!*

I heard about a guy who married his ex-wife's sister. He figured it would be too tough to break in a new mother-in-law.

29

USHER AT WEDDING: Are you a friend of the groom?
LADY AT WEDDING: I should say not; I'm the bride's mother!

A man who had just checked out of a hotel room discovered that his umbrella was missing. By the time he got back to the room, it was already occupied by a newly married couple. Listening at the door, he heard the following conversation:

Groom: Whose lovely eyes are those, darling?
Bride: Yours, sweetheart.
Groom: Whose lovely, gorgeous lips are those?
Bride: Yours, lover.
Groom: And whose precious, swan-like neck is that, baby?
Bride: Yours, dearest.
At this point the man yelled through the key-hole: *When you get to the umbrella . . . it's mine!*

I understand that in Hollywood, the new marriage licenses include a ticket to Reno, with a one-day stopover at Niagara Falls, for a honeymoon.

Dear Advice to the Lovelorn: The other night my boy friend and I were sitting in the parlor when suddenly the light fuse blew out. What would you have done in my case? Signed: Worried.
Dear Worried: I'd have probably done the same thing you did and been twice as worried.

BEDTIME STORY: Once upon a time two concrete mixers fell in love and got married. Now they have a little sidewalk running around the house.

SHE: Before we got married, you told me you were well-off.
HE: I was and I didn't know it.

JUDGE: Young man, you are accused of constantly beating your wife, blacking her eyes, and breaking her nose. What have you to say to her complaint?
MAN: Aww . . . pay no attention to her, Judge, she's *punch-drunk!*

Description of an intimate restaurant: It's the kind of place the boss takes his wife when he doesn't want his secretary to see 'em.

A stitch in time is usually a surprise to a married man.

A harassed husband who was worried about bills was walking along the street one night, when suddenly he was accosted by a stick-up man. "Gimmee all your dough, or I'll blow your brains out," said the tough guy. "Start shootin'," said the poor soul. "When you're married you can live without brains, but you gotta have money!"

HUSBAND: Honey, how come it's taking you so long to cook that chicken?
BRIDE: Well, the cook book says to cook one half hour to the pound and I weigh 110 lbs.

"Honey, wake up! There are burglars in the kitchen! I think they're eating the biscuits I baked this morning!"
"What do we care as long as they don't die in the house?"

Advice to girls who are looking for their dream man: Don't wait too long. I know one girl, who waited so long for her ship to come in, her pier collapsed.

PATIENCE

The wedding bells were ringing, and the sky was a lovely
  blue,
The groom was a man of ninety-five; his bride was ninety-
  two,
Her face was so fill'd with wrinkles, you could hardly see
  her smile,
His wheel chair was bright and shiny as he roll'd it down
  the aisle,
Yes, he ninety-five and she ninety-two . . . so let it be
  reported
That here was the one conservative pair that waited till
  they could afford it!

A man told his wife that a mudpack might improve her looks, so she put on a mudpack. It improved her looks so much, she wouldn't take it off for three weeks.

"I've been asked to get married plenty of times."
"Oh yeah? By whom?"
"My father and mother."

When Jayne split up with her fiancé, he demanded his ring back. Just to aggravate him, she returned it in a box marked, "*Glass . . . handle with care.*"

Some guy invented a crazy chain letter. You send your wife along with the names of ten of your friends. When your name gets to the top of the list they send you thirty thousand wives. If you break the chain, you may get your own wife back.

Romance consists of three rings:

> The engagement ring. . . .
> The wedding ring. . . .
> And the suffer-ring.

MARRIAGE: First year . . . he talks; she listens.
Second year . . . she talks; he listens.
Third year . . . they both talk . . . the neighbors
listen.

PERSONAL: To my husband, Joe, who left home during breakfast, three years ago. *Come home . . . your coffee is getting cold.*

A policeman nabbed a couple "necking" in the park and dragged them up in front of the judge. The man explained to the court that it was perfectly okay as the lady was his wife, and the case was dismissed. "I'm sorry," said the arresting cop to the man. "I had no idea the lady was your wife." "Neither did I," whispered the man, "till you flashed that light in our faces."

When a man has two wives, it's called "Bigamy."
When a man has three or more wives, it's called "Polygamy."
When a man has one wife, it's called "Monotony."

Talk about quick thinkers: when the boss's wife walked in and found his attractive secretary sitting on his lap, he looked at the cutie and said, "Miss Jones, shortages or no shortages, we've gotta have more chairs in this office."

Song Title: Since Grandma shot a hole in Grandpa's head, it sure cleared up his sinus.

"What makes you think your wife is getting tired of you?"
"She keeps wrapping my lunch in a roadmap."

While driving down a lonely country road, a couple's car slid off the highway and became imbedded in a muddy ditch. The husband waded out into the mud up to his knees and tried to pry the car loose. His wife stuck her head out the car window and inquired, "Honey, are we stuck in the mud?" "No," replied the aggravated husband, "the motor died and I'm trying to give it a decent burial!"

You can always tell the difference between a single man and a married man. The single man has no buttons on his shirt. The married man . . . no shirt!

"My sister is having trouble with her husband and the furnace."
"What do you mean?"
"When she watches one, the other goes out!"

Joey Adams' lovely wife, Cindy, was telling me about her Aunt Sarah who was known for her frugality. She was giving instructions to Cindy as to how to dispose of her belongings when she passed away. "Now, Cindy," she said, "don't bury me in my best black dress as that would be a total waste. Bury me in my second best and cut out the back so you can use the material to make something

35

nice for yourself." Cindy laughed and replied, "Now Aunt Sarah, you won't want to walk up those Golden Stairs to meet Uncle Ben with the back cut out of your dress. What would the angels say?" "Child," said Aunt Sarah, "they wouldn't say anything, because they'll be too busy looking at Uncle Ben. I buried him without his pants!"

A bachelor is a man who goes to work every day from a different direction.

ADVICE TO WISE GUYS: If you wanna cure yourselves of gambling, get married on a bet.

Isn't it funny how a girl will scream at the sight of a mouse, but she'll think nothing of getting into a car with a wolf.

NEWSPAPER ITEM: A man who speaks ten languages is getting married to a girl who speaks three. (I think that's about the right handicap.)

HUSBAND TO WIFE: The laundry sure goofed; they must have sent me the wrong shirt. This collar is so tight, I can hardly breathe.
WIFE TO HUSBAND: That's not the wrong shirt, stupid, you've got your head through a buttonhole.

Danny Dayton and his lovely wife, the popular TV star, Dagmar, were surprised on their wedding anniversary to find two tickets to a Broadway hit show in their mail. All that the enclosed message read was, "Guess who?" Of course, they went to the Broadway show, and upon returning home, found out their apartment had been robbed and ransacked. On the piano they found a note that said, "Now you know."

BRIDE: Honey, how do you prepare frankfurters?
GROOM: I dunno. I guess the same way you prepare fish.
BRIDE: That's no good. I tried it. Once you clean out those wienies there's nothing left.

CLIPPED FROM THE NEWSPAPERS: A girl was in an automobile accident and had six ribs broken. She sued and collected $50. Another girl sued a rich old guy for a broken heart and collected $50,000. Let that be a lesson to you guys: *Don't fool around with their hearts; kick 'em in the ribs; it's cheaper!*

He had just asked her father for his blessings. "I hope you can support a family," said the "old man." "Oh," replied the prospective son-in-law, "we're not gonna have any family." "Don't be silly," said the father. "You two are young, healthy, you're bound to have children." "I dunno," said the boy, knocking wood. "We've been lucky so far."

SONG TITLE: I'd like to drown my troubles but I can't get my mother-in-law near the water.

A traveling salesman stopped by a farmhouse and asked for a night's lodging. "We're all fill'd up," said the farmer, "but you can sleep with the little redheaded school teacher." "That's all right," said the traveling salesman.

37

"I'm a perfect gentleman." "Fine," said the farmer, "so is the little redheaded schoolteacher!"

My in-laws act like out-laws.

My wife thinks she's a good driver because she can back out of the garage without closing her eyes.

MARRIAGE IN HOLLYWOOD: According to statistics, out of every ten couples married in Hollywood, eight couples get divorced. The other two couples fight it out to the bitter end. One actress has been married so many times she has a charge account at the City Hall. She was introducing her son to her new husband and said, "Honey, say 'hello' to your new Daddy." The kid looked up and said to him, "Would you please write something in my visitor's book?" They also tell about the much-married star who ran to her husband yelling, "Your kids and my kids are fighting with our kids!"

NEWS ITEM: Woman shoots husband with bow and arrow. (She didn't wanna wake the children.)

> Papa loved Mama
> Mama loved men.
> Ma's in the morgue
> Pa's in the pen.

My wife has been spring-cleaning again. My wallet is empty.

Talk about being naive. I was walking down the street with a girl one day, when a dog ran by with a tin-can tied to his tail. She said, "Awww . . . isn't that cute . . . he just got married."

"How long did it take your wife to learn to drive?"
"It'll be ten years next month."

NEWS NOTE: A man was sued for divorce because of reckless driving. He drove by his wife with some blonde.

PEOPLE-ARE-VERY-STRANGE-DEPT.: Some guy who hadn't kissed his wife in five years shot a guy who did.

A man whose wife was a terrible back-seat driver, finally got disgusted and bought a motorcycle with a sidecar. This did not stop his wife from constantly "yakity-yaking." One day, while riding down the street, a speed cop stopped him and said, "Hey, your wife fell out of the sidecar about six blocks back." "Thank God," he replied, "I thought I was going deaf."

"Don't you think that brunettes have sweeter dispositions than blondes or redheads?"
"I can't see the difference, and my wife has been all three."

Talk about being consistent: I heard of a bridegroom who passed phony checks to pay for the wedding ring, the license, and the preacher, and then took his wife on their honeymoon in a stolen car.

He could read his wife like a book, but some of the best chapters were missing.

We were married six months before we went on our honeymoon. When someone asked us why, my wife replied, "We wanted to see how things would work out before we spent the money."

During a week when her husband and all three children were sick at home, a harassed young housewife commented, "The toughest thing about being a wife and mother is . . . you have no place to stay home from."

Marriage begins when you sink in his arms and end up with your arms in the sink.

A woman who was thoroughly disgusted with her husband for constantly getting drunk said to him, "If you get soused once more, you'll turn into a rat." The next night he came home loaded, cautiously approached the butler, and said to him, "If you suddenly see me getting smaller and smaller . . . keep your eye on that cat!"

How Love Can Solve the Unemployment Situation: Put all the unemployed men on one island and all the unemployed women on another island. Think how busy they'll be . . . building boats!

Marriage is wonderful. Without it husbands and wives would have to fight with strangers.

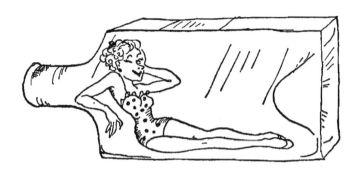

chapter three

BOOZE AND BROADS

(Or: She was luscious. In fact, she was one of the
biggest *lushes in town.*)
(Or: She had a Sunday school face, but she had Satur-
day night ideas.)
(Or: You can't tell how a girl will turn out till her folks
turn in.)
(Or: The Wages of Gin is breath.)

We only had one real bona-fide drinker in our family and
that was my southern uncle, "Uncle Ben." I think his birth
certificate musta been printed on a cork. He was a bottle
baby all his life and when he died, he was so full of
"corn-likker," we hadda shuck him before we could
bury him. I remember he had "patriotic eyes." Blue, with

red whites. He took a blood test once and the doctors offered him $60 a case. He always said he hated the sight of whiskey. "I don't like to look at the stuff," he'd say, "because it makes my mouth water and I don't like to dilute it." He also had a favorite saying, that went, "Liquor kills more people than bullets, but I'd rather be fulla liquor than fulla bullets." Uncle Ben never drank more than he could stand, and the minute he could stand, he'd start drinking again. He even graduated from college, "Magna Cum Loaded." He and my aunt almost didn't get married. They were engaged for thirty years. She wouldn't marry him when he was drunk, and he wouldn't marry her when he was sober. I still don't know how they worked it out. I met him on the street one day, and he told me that he had been "dispossessed." When I asked him, "How come?" he told me they were repairing the gutter. I remember Uncle Ben had one arm longer than the other. His right arm. That was the one the cops used when they dragged him home. One day, he and a bunch of his cronies got loaded and started singing "We won't be home 'till morning." Some cops pinched 'em, and they didn't get home for thirty days. I think I'll dedicate this chapter to Uncle Ben.

> Here's to good old Uncle Ben,
> An astonishing man, I think.
> During his life he spill'd more booze
> Than most people ever drink.

How to Avoid a Hangover: Keep drinking.

43

DOCTOR: I can't find anything wrong with you. I think it's due to drinking.

BOOZER: Okay, Doc, I'll come back when you're sober.

ADVICE TO HANGOVER VICTIMS: Wear a bathing suit to bed, in case your ice bag leaks.

SONG TITLE: Use a bottle opener, Grandma, or you'll ruin your gums.

If all brides are beautiful, where do so many ugly married women come from?

A drunk who was a little more "loaded" than usual was walking along the railroad tracks. After a while he started talking to himself: "This is the longest stairway and the lowest bannister I've ever seen."

Lee Wagner, a friend of mine, tells about the drunk on his way home who accidently found himself at the Park Zoo. He stopped in front of the Hippo cage, looked at the huge beast, and said, "Don't look at me like that, honey, I can explain everything."

"You play beautifully. What made you take up the piano?"

"The glass of beer kept falling off my violin."

She was built like a telephone building. Every line was busy.

44

"Why do you always go out with two girls?"
"In case of a flat tire, it's nice to have a spare."

The reason it takes women longer to dress is because they have to slow down on the curves.

Girls' bathing suits are getting skimpier and skimpier. I saw one the other day that looked like the girl kept it on by suction. It looked like something a silkworm knocked off during his lunch hour. All I know is that if she ever has her appendix taken out, and she doesn't want the scar to show, they'll have to take it out through her nose!

HOUSE DETECTIVE: (Knocking on door) Hey, have you got a girl in your room?
MAN'S VOICE: Yeah . . . what about it?
HOUSE DETECTIVE: Okay, we thought you were a sissy!

CHEMICAL ANALYSIS OF WOMEN

Symbol: WO
Accepted atomic weight: About 112 lbs.
Occurrence: Found wherever man exists. Seldom in the free state.
Physical properties: Boils at nothing, and may freeze at any minute. Melts when properly treated. Very bitter if not well used.
Chemical properties: Very active. Possesses great affinity for gold, silver, platinum, and precious stones. Violent

45

reaction when left alone. Able to absorb great amounts of expensive food. Turns green when placed beside a better looking specimen. Ages rapidly.

Uses: Highly ornamental. Useful as a tonic in acceleration of low spirits, etc. Equalizes distribution of wealth. Is probably the most powerful income reducing agent known.

CAUTION: Highly explosive when in inexperienced hands.

A man is known by the company he thinks nobody knows he's keeping.

A man celebrates his birthday by taking a day off. A woman takes a year off.

"See that gorgeous babe over there. She's been aggravating me all evening."

"Aggravating you? She hasn't even looked at you."

"I know, that's what's aggravating me."

STUDENT: Hy'a, Coach.

PROF: Don't you know you're not supposed to drink while you're in training?

STUDENT: What maksh you think I've been drinking?

PROF: Because I'm not the coach!

A drunk in a bar raised his glass in a "toast" and said, "Good night, Marilyn Monroe . . . *wherever I am!*"

A local newspaper got a call from a woman who

wanted her husband's name put in the obituary column because she found him cheating with his secretary. When the editor asked how long the man had been dead, she replied, "He starts tomorrow."

"Doctor, I'm seventy years old and I think it's about time I got married and raised a family. I should have an heir."

"At seventy? I'm sorry; you may be heir-minded, but you're not heir-conditioned."

FIRST GIRL: When John took me home, he kissed me and woke up the whole family.
SECOND GIRL: Did he kiss you against your will?
FIRST GIRL: No, against the doorbell!

"Booze and gasoline don't mix," they say. They *do*, but they taste lousy.

Some guy just invented a perfume that'll drive the women crazy. It smells like money.

SONG TITLE: When skirts look shorter, the men look longer.

A man in the furniture business was telling his friend about his trip to Paris. "So I meet this little French broad," he says, "and we go out to dinner. Well, she can't talk English, and I can't talk French. After dinner, she takes a pencil and draws a picture of a bed on the tablecloth. You know, to this day I dunno how she figured out I was in the furniture business."

47

OH HENRY LET'S NOT PARK HERE.
OH HENRY LET'S NOT PARK
OH HENRY LET'S NOT
OH HENRY LET'S
OH HENRY
OH.

ROAD SIGNS: Dangerous curves.
Soft shoulders.
Men at work.
Beware children.

Sign on store: LADIES READY TO WEAR CLOTHES. (I think it's about time.)

SONG TITLE: Since you stopped wearing low-cut dresses, I see your eyes are blue.

THE GEOGRAPHY OF WOMEN

From 17 to 25 women are like Africa: part virgin and part explored.

From 25 to 35 women are like the U.S.: high-toned and temperate.

From 35 to 45 they are like Asia: dark and mysterious.

From 45 to 55 they are like Europe: devastated but interesting in places.

From 55 to ? They are like Australia: everybody knows where it is, but very few people go there.

"How's your wife?"
"Better than nothing."

48

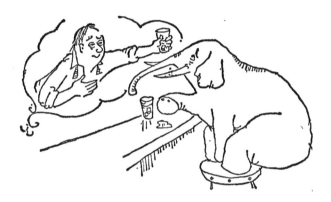

Bartender talking to Pink Elephant: "I'm sorry, but Joe hasn't been here yet."

A couple wanted to get married in a hurry. The man, a soldier on a forty-eight hour pass, took his bride to the minister. "Impossible," said the clergyman, "even a special license would take too long." "Well," suggested the soldier, "couldn't you just say a few words to tide us over the week-end?"

A drunk wandered into a barber shop. His hat was pulled down almost over his ears. "Gimmie a haircut," he said. "You'll have to take your hat off," the barber told him. "Oh excuse me," he replied, "I didn't know there were ladies present."

A woman never forgets her age . . . once she's decided on it.

GUY: Where'll we go?
GAL: Let's go to my house.
GUY: Are your mother and father home?
GAL: Nope.
GUY: Is your brother home?
GAL: Nope. Nobody's home.
GUY: Who'll we talk to?

A highly-publicized Hollywood "sex-pot" was stopping at a New York hotel. She had just stepped out of the bathtub, and was reaching for a towel, when she noticed a window washer at the window. At the same moment, he happened to look in at her. The glamor girl, too paralyzed to move, kept staring at the window washer. "Whatchas lookin' at," he drawled. "Aintcha never seen a window washer before?"

The horse and mule live thirty years and never know of wines and beers.

The goat and sheep at twenty die and never know of scotch or rye.

The cow drinks water by the ton, and at eighteen years is mostly done.

The dog at sixteen cashes in without the aid of rum or gin.

The cat in milk and water soaks . . . and then at twelve short years, it croaks.

The modest, sober, bone-dry hen, lays eggs for nogs then dies at ten.

All animals are strictly dry, they sinless live and swiftly die.

But sinful, ginful, rum-soaked men survive for three score years and ten.

And some of them, a very few, stay pickled till they're ninety-two.

—Anonymous

Overheard through the transom of a hotel doorway: "John, you never used to smoke in bed before we were married."

Firemen, pulling drunk out of a burning bed: "You darned fool, that'll teach you to smoke in bed."

Drunk: "I wasn't smoking in bed. It was on fire when I laid down."

My girl has one red eye and one green eye. I don't know whether to stop or go ahead.

They always say, "Be ready when opportunity knocks."
Well, one night I was ready, when somebody knocked and
spoiled a beautiful opportunity.

"Gimme a cuppa coffee and a bun."
"We don't have any buns."
"Okay, then I'll jusht have a cuppa tea and a bun."
"I don't think you heard me . . . we don't have any buns."
"I ain't one of them drunks gonna make you trouble,
    Buddy, I'll just have a glassa milk and a bun."
"You jerk, don't you understand . . . we have no buns . . .
    no buns!"
"If you're gonna get sore . . . I'll just have a bun."

A housewife, wanting to relax a little from the chores
of the day, took a quick shot of bourbon. She still had the
odor of the liquor on her breath as she kissed her little
girl good night. "Gee, Mommy," the kid said, "I didn't
know you used Daddy's perfume."

"My girl friend is a twin."
"How do you tell 'em apart?"
"Her brother is built different."

It was Eli Whitney who said, "Keep your cotton-pickin'
hands off my gin."

"Oh . . . you're just like all the rest of the men."
"I hope so."

NEWS ITEM: Big fire at burlesque show. (It took one hour to put out the fire, and three hours to put out the firemen.)

"I will now play the Hungarian Rhapsody by Goulash."
"Goulash is a stew."
"I don't care how much he drinks; he writes good music."

A drunk walked into a bar, put a dime on the counter, and asked for a glass of whiskey. "We don't sell any dime whiskey," said the bartender. "Well," said the drunk, "if you think I'm gonna drink any of that nickel stuff, you're nuts."

"Whatever happened to that stupid blonde your husband used to run around with?"
"I dyed my hair."

This girl had some shape. Every brick in place!

"On the bus today, I hadda change my seat four times."
"Some guy get fresh?"
"Yeah, finally."

A drunk who was hungry, walked into the Automat, put ten dollars in nickels and dimes into the slots, and had his table piled up with food. The manager walked over and said to him, "Come on, get out of here, Buddy, you're drunk." "Oh no you don't," replied the lush. "Not when I'm winning."

COP: Come on, Buddy, move along.
DRUNK: I live here, offisher.
COP: Why don't you go in the house?
DRUNK: I forgot my key, wise guy.
COP: Why don't you ring the bell?
DRUNK: I rang the bell a half hour ago and nobody answered.
COP: Why don't you ring it again?
DRUNK: To Hell with 'em! *Let 'em wait!*

A drunk watching a revolving door, saw a man walk in, and a few seconds later, a pretty girl stepped out. "It's a good trick," he said, "but I still don't know what she did with the guy's clothes."

SONG TITLE: I found a million-dollar baby, but after taxes she wasn't worth a dime.

Two drunks were seated on bar stools drinking constantly. Finally, one of them named Harry turned and fell flat on his face . . . out cold. His friend looked down at him, then said to the bartender, "That's what I like about Harry; he knows when he's had enough."

The trouble with those sultry lasses
Is that they always steam your glasses.

Lady Godiva was quite a gal. When she rode down the streets of Coventry, you could hear the men yelling, "Hooray for our side." When she got home, her husband

54

asked, "Where the *hell've* ya been? The horse got home two hours ago."

In Puerto Rico, they raise cane to make rum. Then they drink rum to raise Cain!

A drunk who had just fallen out of a three-story window regained consciousness to see a big crowd gathered around him. A policeman asked him, "What happened?" "I dunno," replied the drunk. "I just got here!"

Talk about the hardy people of the old West; one day a man, his wife, and small son walked into a saloon. "Give us two whiskeys" said the man. "Wassa matter, Pop?" asked the kid, "Ain't Maw drinkin'?"

Our grand piano is so old only half the keys are left. When you play "Cocktails for Two," it comes out, "Short Beer for One."

How to Get the Cherry Out of a Highball Glass

Number one: Cautiously push your spoon down through the myriad particles of ice and fruitskins toward the cherry. Having reached the bottom of the glass, give aforementioned spoon a forward shove. This will cause much of the ice to jump out of the glass onto the floor. Leave the ice there, as one never knows when there may be a midget ice skater around who will be grateful for this added chance of getting in a little blade cutting. Other-

wise disregard the ice, and look at the people at the next table as if they did it.

Number two: Have the spoon approach the cherry with deliberation, but with caution, so as not to arouse the cherry's suspicion. Then, make a sudden lunge. If you do not have the cherry by this time, try the following:

Number three: Drink the lemonade, orangeade, coke, highball, or whatever is in the glass, then take each piece of ice out of the glass individually. Next, thrust your two longest fingers down about the fruit peelings, and work around until you encounter the cherry. After you have squashed the cherry beyond recognition, you *may* get it out. If not, try the following:

Number four: Eat all the fruit skins in the glass. Then, turn the glass upside down with the mouth touching your lips. Give the bottom of the glass a healthy tap. The cherry will probably bounce out on your nose and land on the floor. If not, and it still remains in the glass, try the following:

Number five: BREAK THE GLASS! Somewhere among the shattered pieces, you will find the cherry. Simple isn't it? (If you've followed the above . . . *so are you!*)

chapter four

THICK AND THIN

(Or: She was so fat, she had to put on a girdle to get into a kimono.)
(Or: He was so skinny his muscles looked like fleabites on a piece of spaghetti.)

They say a boy becomes a man when he stops growing up and down, and starts growing sideways. That's what happened to me. I developed what is called "sandwich-spread." It's something you get from eating between meals. I ate like a horse. Soon I began to look like one. The doctor told me to watch my stomach, which was easy, as there it was in front of me all the time. I started

looking like an ad for "What time does the balloon go up?"
When I sat down on a bar stool, I had a hangover. Even
my legs were so fat, I had to "jack" 'em apart to get my
pants on. It affected my golf game. When I put the ball
where I could see it, I couldn't hit it . . . and when I put the
ball where I could hit it . . . I couldn't see it. I became a
real glutton and I finally got a black eye from overeating. I
ate more than I could pay for.

The doctor put me on a nine-day diet. I ate the whole
thing in one meal and didn't lose an ounce. Then he said,
"Whenever you get hungry, instead of eating, drink some
water." I drank so much water my stomach started going
in and out with the tide. I saw an ad for reducing pills. I
ate four boxes and gained five pounds. Then I found out
what the trouble was. I should have been eating the pills
instead of the boxes. These pills didn't curb your appetite,
they poisoned the food. They were $8 a dozen, including
stomach pump! Suddenly, I found the magic word for
losing weight. *Starvation!* The first week, I lost one inch
off my waistline . . . the second week, I lost two inches off
my waistline . . . the third week, I lost my jockey shorts!

And that's why I say: Some guy oughta invent a No-Cal
hair tonic for fatheads!

She had a shape like the coastline of New Jersey, but
she was a little plump around Bayonne.

"My brother has a big stomach, but he says he's gonna
  diet."
"What color?"

I know a guy who's so skinny and emaciated looking, the only way he can get any color in his face, is to stick his tongue out!

They say fat people are good-natured. They *have* to be good-natured. They're too heavy to run and too fat to fight!

> I had an aunt named Sadie,
> She was so darned stout,
> They hadda put sand on her bed sheets,
> To keep her from rolling out.

Wear Irish girdles. They're so tight, you'll turn green!

"I understand your brother got very thin."
"He sure did. Remember that big Mack truck he had tattooed on his stomach?"
"Yeah."
"Well it's now a Volkswagen!"

Artie Nardin who owns some of the world's top harness race horses says that a horse's diet is very important too. He explains that race horses don't eat the day before a race. I know lots of bettors that don't eat for days afterwards.

The husband of a very fat woman was telling his friend that he was taking his wife to the mountains for a few days. His friend inquired, "For resting or grazing?"

On a streetcar one day, I noticed a big, fat woman sitting there crying. When I asked her what was wrong, she replied, "I've gone eight blocks past my station. You see I'm so fat I have to back off the streetcar, and everytime I do, someone thinks I'm getting on and pushes me back into the car!"

"I've got a cousin who weighs four hundred pounds and you should see her dance the Hula-Hula."
"How can a woman weighing four hundred pounds do the Hula?"
"Easy . . . she runs a few feet . . . stops suddenly . . . and lets Nature take its course!"

I know a lady who has so many double chins she needs a bookmark to find her necklace. When she drives over car tracks, her double chins applaud . . . and with her big ears . . . from the back, she looks like a taxi with both doors open!

It was Sam Levenson who originated this famous line about dieting. "Eat all you want . . . chew . . . but don't swallow!"

> My brother's wife is so skinny
> That when she puts on a strapless gown,
> She has to wear suspenders
> To keep it from falling down.

A fat man was kidding his skinny friend: "From the looks of you, people would think we had a famine." "Oh yeah," replied the thin one, "and from the looks of you, they'd think you caused it!"

A very fat girl who was also very religious, when she couldn't get a brassiere large enough for her needs was heard to mutter, "My cup runneth over."

"I'm getting so thin, you can count my ribs."
"Gee, thanks."

I knew my wife was getting too thin when we walked into a restaurant one day, arm in arm, and the headwaiter said, "You'll have to check your umbrella."

I'll never forget my cousin Pearl. Everything I said to her went in one head and out the other. That's right, she had two heads, and I've never seen anyone eat like she did. Eat, eat, eat, all the time. Finally, one day I said to her, "You should be ashamed of yourself, you're a glutton!" So she hung one head in shame, but with the other head, she kept right on eating!

I wouldn't exactly say that my uncle is overweight, but you know those "Talking Scales," that have a recorded device that speaks your weight? When he got on, it said, "One at a time, please." He's so fat that, when he gets into a phone booth, he can't get out. And when you can't get out of a phone booth, there's no use talking. He took up horseback riding to lose weight. The horse is now so "sway-back" he has to walk on tiptoes to keep his stomach from dragging!

62

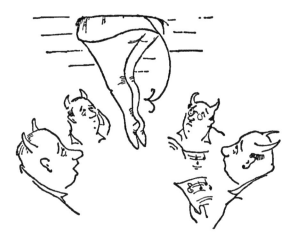

They tell a story in one of the famous opera houses about the time that Lauritz Melchior was singing the role of the Devil in the opera "Faust." At one point in the performance, where he is supposed to descend into Hades, the trap door was not big enough to allow his portly figure to pass through. There he was, stuck between the stage floor and basement. After the first hysterics of the audience had died down, a voice from the balcony was heard to yell, "What's the matter, Melchior . . . are they all fill'd up down there?" (Okay, so Melchior *is* a tenor. It's a good story anyway.)

63

A little girl was warned to be on her best behavior, so her mother was quite upset when the child asked a caller her age. "Oh, I'm just as old as your Mommy," was the reply. The little girl made a quick appraisal of the "over-stuffed" guest and said, "My, you're large for your age, aren't you?"

SONG TITLE: "Grandma, don't throw away your old corset; we can use it for a hammock on the back porch."

"Lookit that skinny guy."
"Yeah, if he was alive, he'd be a very sick man."

"The doctor told me that exercise is an important part of weight control, so this morning, I put my hands over my head, bent over, and jumped six feet into the air."
"Was that part of the exercise?"
"No, but when I bent over, I backed into a hot radiator!"

chapter five

DOCTORS

(Or: "Before you operate, show me your operator's
license!")
(Or: "Have forceps, will travel.")
(Or: "May I cut in?")

My doctor is a genius. He's performed over four hundred
operations and never cut himself once. He's a bone specialist. Carries his own dice. He's also a little absent-minded.
Once, he sewed up an incision and left his rubber gloves
in the patient. To this day, when the guy meets him on
the street, his stomach shakes hands. When you go to his
office, he has a little card for you, and on this card is

printed all the diseases known to medical science. As he examines you, he punches a little hole in the card, right next to whatever your trouble is. I took my card home, put it on the player piano, and it played, "So Long, It's Been Good to Know You!"

He has no conscience when it comes to bills. He got sick once and wouldn't treat himself. He charges too much. Once, when I had a sore throat, he painted it with silver nitrate. Big deal! Musta cost him about 14¢. He sent me a bill for $175. How do you like that? $175 for painting my throat. For another three bucks, I coulda had an original Picasso! I wrote him a note and told him his bill got me so mad it made my blood boil . . . so he charged me another fifty for sterilizing my system!

I can't fight with him, though, because he's such a wonderful doctor. He even cured a man of drinking, by an operation. He removed a brass rail that had been pressing against the guy's foot! He grafted a smile onto a jackass and got a Congressman! Another guy had his eyebrows burnt off in a fire and my doctor grafted new eyebrows on him. He took the hair from the hind leg of a cocker spaniel. Of course, this left the patient with a little problem. Everytime he passes a hydrant, *he looks "surprised"!*

Speaking of doctors:
"Oh, Doctor, Doctor . . . I broke my glasses. Do I have to be examined all over?"
"No, just your eyes."

Dear Doctor: I was deaf for twelve years, but since using your wonderful ear oil, I heard from my brother in Nebraska.

After seven face-lift jobs during a period of five years, an aging actress was asked by her doctor how she felt. "Well, doctor," she answered, "I feel fine, except everytime I raise my eyebrows I pull up my stockings."

"My doctor put me on a garlic diet."
"Did you lose weight?"
"No, friends."

Dear Doctor: May I compliment you on your wonderful new medicine. I had a boil on the back of my neck that was so big, when I went to sleep at night, I had to rest the boil on a chair next to the bed. After taking only six bottles of your fine elixir, I now sleep on the floor, and the boil sleeps in bed!

"Doctor, Doctor, I'm so nervous. This is my first operation."
"I know just how you feel. You're my first patient!"

DOCTOR TO PATIENT: Here are three pills, two green ones and a red one. Take the two green pills first.
PATIENT TO DOCTOR: What's the red one for?
DOCTOR TO PATIENT: In case the green ones are poison!

A doctor, looking at his own wife's X-rays, was heard to remark: "You know, she looks just like her mother."

Which reminds me of the doctor who knew his patient couldn't afford an operation, so he "retouched" his X-rays.

"I was up all last night with a sick friend."

"Who was he?"

"I dunno . . . he was too sick to tell me."

I see in the papers that some drunk was arrested for performing an illegal operation. He opened a guy's head with a beer bottle.

Some doctor just invented a new miracle drug that is so powerful, you have to be in perfect health to use it.

I think it was the same doctor, who invented the remedy for an ailment that cures a disease for which there is no sickness!

I knew a guy who doctored himself out of a medical book for twelve years. He finally died of a typographical error.

DENTIST: Open wide. Wider . . . *wider!*

PATIENT: Doc . . . are you gonna look in or walk in?

HOW TO AVOID CATCHING COLD: Don't breathe in public. Don't fall asleep in the yard with the gate open. Don't drink out of damp glasses.

NEWS NOTE: *Woman Gives Birth to Twins on Subway.* (Pretty sneaky way to get a seat.)

68

"I'm gonna have a party to celebrate the arrival of our
new baby."

"Swell. I'll bring the cigars."

"Oh, no you don't. No kid of mine is gonna smoke."

"My doctor sure put me back on my feet."

"Really?"

"Yeah, when I got his bill, I hadda sell my car!"

An old doctor was dictating his will to his attorney. He said, "To my daughter, I leave one hundred thousand dollars. To my son, I leave one hundred thousand dollars and to their children, ten thousand dollars each. And to my nephew who always says that *'Health is better than wealth,'* I leave my sun lamp!"

Dr.: I told you to eat only such things as could be digested by a three-year-old."

Mr.: I did. A handful of mud . . . some orange peels, two buttons, and a rusty nail.

A friend of mine is such a hypochondriac, he found a feather in his bed and thought he had *chicken-pox*.

In answer to a frantic call from a father-to-be, a doctor grabbed his little black bag and rushed to the home of the expectant mother. "Where's your wife?" the Doc asked the man. "She's upstairs, Doctor, please hurry!" The Doc, the little black bag and all, rushed up the stairs, only to return a few seconds later and ask the man, "Do you have a pair of pliers?" The man gave him a pair of pliers and the doctor rushed upstairs again. A few minutes later, the doctor was back downstairs again, this time asking the poor man for a screw-driver and a monkey-wrench. The almost-new Father was in a panic. "How's my wife?" he demanded. "Your wife?" screamed the doctor. "Who knows about your wife? *I'm still trying to open up my little black bag!*"

"You're dancing with me tonight, but tomorrow you'll probably make a date with some other man."
"Yeah, the foot-doctor."

A sailor friend of mine had the British Navy tattooed on his stomach. When the doctor took his appendix out, he sank two battleships, three rowboats, and a small "dingy."

My good friend Harvey Stone tells about the girl who told the plastic-surgeon she wanted a "turned-up" nose. Evidently, the doctor turned it up too far. Everytime she sneezes, she blows her hat off!

Doc: You're not getting any younger, you know. You should start leading a quiet life. The best thing for you is to cut out late hours, liquor, and women.
Pat: Doc, I don't really deserve the best. What's next best?

"I was just reading a newspaper in my doctor's office."
"What's new?"
"McKinley was assassinated."

A "Specialist" is a doctor who diagnoses your case by feeling your purse.

About My Dentist: He checked my mouth over the other day and told me that my teeth were in perfect shape . . . but he'd have to take out my gums! There's a guy who gets a drill in his hand and gets drunk with power. One day, he was drilling away on one of my back teeth for about an hour. Finally he looks at me, as if it was my fault and says, "You've had this tooth fill'd before." "I have not," I told him. "Yes, you have," he insisted. "I been drilling here and I found something red, something green, and something yellow." I told him, *"You darned fool . . . you're down to my argyle socks!"*

I once had a beautiful nurse and she *knew* she was beautiful. Everytime she took my temperature, she knocked off ten degrees for personality.

I once had an ugly nurse. She had enough wrinkles in her face to hold a two-day rain. In trying to get her attention one day, I pressed the buzzer next to my bed for about a half hour. She finally showed up and inquired, "Did you ring?" "No," I replied, "I was tolling the bell. I thought you were dead!"

Did you hear about the actor who became a famous surgeon? He performed a delicate brain operation in front of a group of internes and nurses. When the operation was completed, the students burst into a tremendous round of applause . . . so . . . for an encore, he took out the patient's appendix.

"Doctor, Doctor! My son just swallowed a fountain pen
    . . . what should I do?"
"Use a pencil."

If rubbing liniment on your arm makes it smart . . . rub some on your head!

One "head-shrinker" out in Los Angeles calls himself the "Friendly Psychiatrist." He lies down on the couch with you. I think they call this "socialized medicine."

I once saw a psychiatrist walking down the street with a couch on his back. Before I could ask him why, he told me: *"I'm making a house call."*

"My doctor is a plastered surgeon."
"You mean *plastic* surgeon, you don't know the expression."
"I mean *'plastered,'* you don't know my doctor."

Did you know that a "psycho-ceramic" is a crack-pot?

Doctors say that sunshine cures internal ailments. Can't you just see your liver hanging out on the line?

Silly sign in hospital: TODAY . . . REMOVAL SALE
                    TONSILS $50.00
                    APPENDIX $60.00
                    LIVER $100.00
                        (with onions, $200.00)

My brother is a "gossiper" in a hospital. He puts people on the pan.

Everybody is diet conscious. Jack E. Leonard tells about the little kid who came up to him one day and asked, "Mister, would you like to lose 20 lbs. of ugly fat?" When he said "yes," the kid came back with, "Cut your head off!"

I knew a fellow who went on one of those "fad" diets. He weighed 350 lbs. Eight weeks later, he weighed 85 lbs. . . . *casket and all!*

My doctor says the best way to lose weight is this exercise. When offered a second helping . . . move the head slowly from left to right.

Then there's the "Rockefeller Diet." For six months, you eat nothing but money. Or the "Thomas Edison Diet." For six months, you eat nothing but light bulbs. You don't take off any weight, but at night, they can see you for miles!

74

Max Asnus, of N. Y.'s famous Stage Delicatessen, says, "The best way to lose weight is to eat all you want of everything you don't like."

A man explained to his psychiatrist that he had a strange psychosis. "At night when I get in bed," he said, "I imagine there is someone under the bed. Then, when I get under the bed, I imagine there is someone on top of the bed. All night long . . . on the bed . . . under the bed . . . it's driving me nuts!" The psychiatrist thought a moment, then said, "I can help you. Come here three times a week, fifty dollars a visit, and in four years, I'll have you cured." The patient told the doctor, "I can't afford that kind of money. I'll have to think it over." A week later, the doctor saw the man on the street and asked why he hadn't come back to the office. "Who needs you?" the man said. "My wife cured me for nothing." "How?" asked the psychiatrist. His quick answer was, "She told me to cut the legs off the bed!"

chapter six

TRANSPORTATION:
Automobiles, Bicycles, Piggy-back, etc.

(Or: You can always tell a new car, by the old one
pushing it.)
(Or: Isn't life colorful? The traffic lights turn red and
green and the pedestrians turn black and blue.)

I always go to the Auto Show. I like to see what's gonna
knock me down next year. I just look, I don't buy. I'm very
happy with the car I have now. Two more payments and
I'll be able to drive it in the daytime. It's a convertible.
If you're driving along with the top down and it starts
raining, you just push a button. The top doesn't go up,
but it stops raining. It's one of those low, underslung
jalopies. In fact, it's built so close to the ground, if you

76

wanna get into the back seat, you have to come up through a manhole. My car is what they call a five-passenger job. One drives and four push. You have to shift gears to get over streetcar tracks. I think its a Lincoln. It has a sign on back that reads "Lincoln. Vote for Lincoln!" It may not be a new car, but it has all the modern inconveniences: disappearing headlights (they disappeared ten years ago), an automobile choke for back-seat drivers, and shatter-proof glass. That shatterproof glass is great stuff. Years ago, when you got into an accident, the glass would break, and you'd get cut all over. Not today . . . *one piece.* ! ! That's all, brother! My car has another gadget that comes in handy, when you run over a pedestrian. It sprinkles peni-cillin out of the exhaust pipe and drops a "get-well" card on his chest. It's also equipped with Radar which comes in very handy when you're out driving with a girl. Radar finds a parking place; Radar turns on the radio; Radar turns off the lights . . . and if you need Radar from then on . . . *you shoulda stayed home!!*

Speaking of automobiles: my pal, Herkie Styles, a comic with a "wild" sense of humor, after admiring a new car in the window of a downtown auto agency, went inside and bought the car.

"Would you like to take it with you now?" the salesman beamed at him.

"No," said Herkie, "I'll just let it stay here. I'll never find another parking place this good."

A parking space is that area that disappears while you are making a U-turn.

Apartment house sign: "No baby carriages or foreign cars allowed in the lobby."

Henny Youngman tells about those new small cars being very dangerous. He says he was driving an MG, put out his hand to turn a corner, and ruptured a policeman.

Calling car 32 . . . calling car 32 . . . wipe off your windshield . . . someone is stealing your radiator cap!

STATISTICS: A man is knocked down by a car every five minutes. The guy must be made of iron.

Don't drive with one arm around your girl. Let her drive and you use both arms.

People who can't pass their driving license tests become parking lot attendants.

"Why do you ride your horse backwards?"
"It makes him nervous to have anyone look over his shoulder."

I guess the reason there are less train accidents than auto accidents is because you never hear about the engineer driving with his arm around the fireman.

A drunk who was accused of stealing a car came up with this ridiculous excuse: "I didn't steal the car, Judge. I saw it parked in front of a cemetery and I thought the owner was dead."

After following a woman driver, who had her hand stuck out of her car for about six blocks, a man pulled up alongside her and said. "For gosh sakes, lady, if you're gonna turn . . . *turn!*" She replied, "Who's turning? I'm drying my nails!"

Did you hear about the Texan who walked into an automobile agency and said to the salesman, "I'd like to get my wife a get-well car."

Those foreign cars are getting so small, I put out my hand to turn a corner and one of 'em ran up my sleeve.

Also about small cars: They used to run over people, now they run under 'em.

I figured out that the bus that stopped at every hydrant must have been a Greyhound.

It was a beautiful day, and I had the top down on my convertible. I was wearing a bright red beret and all of a sudden a cop stopped me. "What's the idea, officer?" I asked. "I wasn't speeding." "I know it," the cop replied. "I saw the beret, and I just wanted to hear you talk."

New Traffic Rules: Any car going down Broadway, over sixty miles per hour, must have a driver.

"I saved four lives today."
"How?"
"I wouldn't let my wife take the car."

After going thru a red light, going the wrong way on a one-way street, jumping the curb, and knocking down a telephone pole, a policeman asked a woman driver for her license. "Don't be silly," she told him. "Who would give me a license?"

Apropos of the above, another woman driver was stopped for speeding. She explained to the policeman, "I'm such a terrible driver, officer, I was hurrying to get home before I killed somebody."

A train engineer got up one morning and in tying his shoes, broke a string. He put salt instead of sugar into his coffee. He missed his bus to work by fifteen seconds. When he got to the round house he put his overalls on backwards. He finally got into his engine and was barreling along about 70 miles an hour. When he glanced out of the cab of his locomotive, he saw another train coming at him head on, at seventy miles an hour on the same track. He turned to the fireman and asked, "Did you ever get one of those days when just *everything goes wrong?*"

A small boy was annoying everyone in the airplane by running up and down the aisle, yelling, pulling pillows out from under the heads of sleeping passengers, and, in general, making an awful fuss. One of the passengers complained to the stewardess. A few minutes later, all was quiet. "How did you do it?" the passenger asked the stewardess. "It was easy," she replied. "I just told the kid to go outdoors and play."

A cab driver who knocked down a pedestrian was being bawled out by a cop. "Wassamatter," the officer yelled, "ya blind?" "Wassamatter," replied the cabbie, "I hit her, didn't I?"

STATISTICS: Out of every four cars in the world, three are in the United States. In Los Angeles alone, there are twice as many cars as in all of South America. Chicago and New York have three times as many cars as Germany and France put together. There is only one solution to this problem; if it gets any worse, we'll all have to park over-seas.

Once upon a time, there was a very beautiful young girl . . . and once upon a time, there was a very handsome young man . . . and once upon a time, this good-looking guy took this lovely girl for a ride in his car. All of a sudden, something went wrong with the motor. The handsome young man jumped out of the car, fixed the motor, jumped back in again, and took the beautiful young girl back home to her parents safe and sound . . . *once upon a time.* See, girls? The moral of the story is: *Never go riding with a mechanic.*

A friend of mine invented a new type of electric automobile. It cost him $4000 to drive it from New York to California—$5 for electricity, and $3995 for the extension cord.

I'm worried about my car. If I don't trade it in pretty soon, I'll own the darned thing.

Sometimes the police can be very unfair. A man who was hit by a car and knocked twenty feet into the air was arrested for leaving the scene of an accident.

ADVICE FROM AN AUTO-MECHANIC: If your brakes don't work . . . try to run into something cheap.

Two fellows were out riding on a motorcycle. The man riding in back asked the driver to stop as he was cold. So he took off his leather jacket and put it on backwards to protect his neck from the wind. They then proceeded along the highway at a fast speed, when suddenly they shot off the road and into a tree. In reporting the accident, the policeman told his superiors, "The first guy was killed outright, but the guy in back was fine . . . that is . . . till we tried to turn his head back around."

I was in one town where the policemen were so polite. I put out my hand to turn a corner and a cop kissed it.

Another time, I was going along "pretty good" when a polite cop pulled me over and said, "You were going sixty miles an hour." "No, I wasn't, officer," I replied. "I wasn't even going fifty . . . in fact I doubt if I was doing more than twenty-five." So he gave me a ticket for parking.

A taxi was standing in front of the City Hall. Suddenly, two midgets who had just gotten married rushed out and jumped into his cab. The little man said to the cabbie, "Turn on the radio, pull down the shades, and just keep driving." After a while, the cabbie's curiosity got the better of him, and he pulled the shade to one side, and peeked into the back seat. What do you think the midgets were doing? They were dancing. (Nyaaa!)

Summer is the time for those week-end auto trips. One day driving, two days folding the road map.

My car has no speedometer and my friends ask me how I can tell what speed I'm doing. Easy. At twenty miles per hour, the fenders rattle, at thirty the doors rattle, and at forty, *I* rattle!

"How come the right side of your car is painted yellow and the left side is painted red?"
"I know it doesn't look good, but in case of an accident, you should hear the witnesses contradict each other."

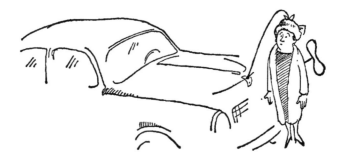

The motor vehicle department has just announced that starting the first of the year, all motorists will have their pedestrians assigned to them.

84

A man driving a horse and wagon approached the toll gate of a bridge. "That'll be fifty cents," said the attendant. "But I thought," said the man, "that was only for motor vehicles." "No," the tollkeeper told him, "That's for any kind of vehicle." The man turned his horse and wagon around, went a few feet back down the road, and got off. He then proceeded to put the horse in the wagon, and started to pull the horse and wagon over the bridge. "That'll be fifty cents," the tollgate keeper said again, at which the man with the horse in the wagon replied, "Talk to the driver."

"Help me, I was just struck by a hit-and-run driver!"
"Has the insurance man been here yet?"
"No."
"Move over!"

My girl had only one eye. Her mother was scared by a motorcycle.

A crowded bus came to a stop to take another passenger aboard. "Wassamatter, Noah?" asked the wise guy of the already-irritated bus driver, "Is the Ark all filled up?" "No," replied the bus driver, "there's room for a jackass! Hop in."

I just got a "Golden Letter" from the Auto Finance Co. It's their fiftieth request for money.

The New York traffic is very musical. If you do not C sharp, you will B flat.

85

"How did you puncture your tire?"
"I ran over a milk bottle."
"Didn't you see it?"
"The man had it in his coat pocket."

A tree is a solid thing that stands for fifty years and then suddenly jumps out in front of a woman driver.

I know my uncle is an idiot. He thinks the white line down the middle of the highway is for bicycles.

It was so hot today, it slowed everybody down. I saw motorists *pushing* their cars over pedestrians.

On the subway the other morning, some crazy man was running around, yelling, *"I'm George Washington . . . I'm George Washington!"* Everybody got panicky, but I saved the day. I yelled, *"Next stop Valley Forge!"* and he got right off.

chapter seven

SPORTS

(Or: They laughed when they saw me in my tight bathing trunks, but when I bent over, they split.)
(Or: The only bad thing about being a good sport is:
you have to lose to be one.)

When I first became an athlete, I started at the bottom.
I had athlete's foot. I was never what you'd call just a
good athlete, or a fair athlete. Let's face it, I was lousy! At
college, the coach made me his assistant. That was the only
way he could keep me off the team. I was string changer

87

on the Yo-yo squad! In football, I played drawback, although I was seriously hurt during one game. I fell off the bench! I sat on the bench so long, I became a very calloused young man. Then I got on the boxing team. I was knocked out fifteen times. Twice while "shadowboxing." I'll never forget my last boxing match. In the third round, I really had my opponent worried. He thought he had killed me! Between rounds, I asked the coach how I was doing. He said, "awful, but keep swinging . . . the breeze might give him a cold!" The guy I was fighting was a "southpaw." He kept hitting me with "lefts." Left to the body, a left to the head . . . a left to the mid-section. I finally hit myself with a right, just to break the monotony! All of a sudden, he "came up with one from the floor," hit me on the chin . . . and they counted me out while I was still in the air!

So I got on the baseball team. I think I was the "bat boy." Everybody said I was "bats." I was a natural ballplayer; I had a face like a catcher's mitt. One day it happened. The big game of the year. The score was 87 to nothing. (A "pitcher's battle.") I was at bat. I swung at the ball. Then they picked me up and I swung again. Suddenly, there was the resounding crack of the ball striking wood, as it hit me in the head and bounced off. So I joined the swimming team. I came from a family of swimmers (shrimps). My grandfather was the town's best diver. He knew every dive in town. At one time he made a sensational dive from a platform 500 feet high into a tank of water three feet deep. Of course, he got killed, but it was a "beaut." His father was the real diver in the family. He just started at 500 feet into three feet of water.

He dove 750 feet into two feet of water; 1000 feet into one one foot of water; he finally broke the world's record. He dived from the top of the Empire State Building into a bowl of chicken soup! And darned near got killed! Some wise guy left a Matzo ball in there! If you think that's ridiculous, read the following:

"My uncle swam two miles in an hour and a half and he swam back in three minutes.
"How'd he do that?"
"His suspenders got caught on the pier."

Golf is a game where a ball 1½ inches in diameter is placed on a ball 8000 miles in diameter. The object is to hit the small ball without hitting the large one.

"You're a hunter. Tell me, what is the best way to catch a rabbit?"
"Hide in the grass and make a noise like a carrot."

A bunch of kids on the farm were playing football. One of the boys kicked the ball too hard, and it landed in the henyard. The rooster looked at the football and then called all the hens together. "Listen girls," he said, "I'm not complaining; I just want you to see what's being done in other yards."

I'll never forget my first wrestling match,
My opponent was wrapped around my spine,
I got so darned mad that I bit his ear,
Surprise! The ear that I bit . . . *was mine!*

89

GOLF STORY: A new golfer was playing a short hole. He tried to "kill" the ball. What a wallop! The ball hit a tree, bounced off, and hit another tree; then it ricocheted onto a rock and finally landed on the green about three inches from the cup. The golfer looked after it in disgust. "Nuts," he mumbled, "if I'd just hit it a little harder."

A big-game hunter was relating one of his experiences. "There I was in the jungle," he said, "when all of a sudden, this big lion jumps out of the bushes. He jumped completely over me, missing my head by about six feet. I ran about a half mile before I dared to look back. What do you think the lion was doing? *He was practising shorter jumps!*

A hunter in the woods fired several quick shots. All of a sudden, he called out, "Harry . . . Lee . . . Jim . . . Artie . . . are you all right?" They all yelled back that they were fine. "Good," said the hunter, "then I guess I shot a deer!"

A friend of mine who'd had no luck on a fishing trip stopped by the fish market on his way home, and bought a dozen trout. He then asked the fishman to *throw* them to him, one at a time. "What's the idea?" asked the fishman. "Look," said my friend, "when I tell my wife that I catch fish . . . *I catch 'em!*"

Skiing is a colorful sport. You can get black and blue. One day at Lake Placid, I was coming down a long slope when a girl skier fell right on top of me. We remained in this position till we reached the bottom of the hill. At this point, I looked up at her and said, "Lady, you might as well get off . . . this is as far as I go."

A public golf course is a place where you hit a ball . . . and a *picnic* runs out and grabs it!

A foursome was out on the golf course really enjoying a good game. As they reached the fourth hole which bordered along the road leading to the countryside, a funeral procession approached.

One of the golfers removed his hat, and stood silent as the hearse passed by. His friends commented about his gesture of respect and he solemnly replied, "Fellows, I think that's the least I could have done. In four more days, we would have been married thirty-five years."

A friend of mine was out hunting, one day, and just as he bent over to tie his shoestring, a bull moose came charging out of the woods. The moose hit him so hard, my friend is now using his pants for a hall tree.

A hundred years ago today a wilderness was here,
A man with powder in his gun went forth to hunt a deer,
But now the times have changed a lot, along a different
   plan,
A girl with powder on her nose goes forth to hunt a man!

"I have a very unusual dog. He has the head of a collie, the body of an airedale and the tail of a cocker spaniel."
"What kind is he?"
"A mongrel."

A skier who likes to brag a little was telling a friend how well he did in St. Moritz, Switzerland. "Man," he said, "I came down that ski slide and shot into the air so high that . . . well, I turned to the man next to me and said, 'You must be a good skier too.' He replied, 'Who's skiing? I'm flying the mail to London!'"

An American and a Scotchman were out duck hunting. They made a bet on who could kill the most ducks with one bullet. A flock of ducks flew over and the Scotchman took a shot at them. He got nothing. Then the American took his shot at another flock. Four ducks came tumbling down to earth. The Scotchman refused to pay off the bet. He said they would have died from the fall anyway.

A golf pro was fired from his job. All he had "to his name" was his golf outfit: the spiked shoes, checkered hat and jacket, and slacks. He walked the streets for days. He was starving. Talk about tough luck . . . all of a sudden, right there on the street in front of him, he saw an un-used "meal ticket." He got so excited that as he bent down to pick up the meal ticket, he stepped on it with his spiked shoes and punched out every meal in the ticket!

They tell a story at the Belmont Race Track about the horse who trotted up to the two dollar window and told the man he'd like to place a bet on his nose. The ticket-man looked up at the horse in amazement and said to him, "You what?" "Wassamatter," asked the horse, "are you surprised to hear a horse talk?" "No," said the ticket man, "it's just that I don't think you can win!" (I told this story to my dog the other day and he said he thought it was silly to think a horse could talk.)

Did you hear about the man who crossed a chicken with a racing form and it laid odds?

Or about the guy who crossed asparagus with mustard and got hot tips?

Boy, what a mob of people at the beach today. I wanted to go in swimming and I had to dive six times before I hit the water. One near-sighted guy dived off the end of the pier into a rowboat and almost got killed. It was tattooed on a guy's chest!

My son Gregory and I were playing golf with Phil Galvano, the well-known golf pro, and his pretty wife at the Englewood Golf Club in New Jersey. We were on the tenth green, when all of a sudden a golf ball came over the trees and landed right on the green about eight feet from the "cup." We looked around and didn't see anyone, so I said, "Let's give this guy a real thrill," and we put his golf ball right into the "cup." Sure enough, a few minutes later, some guy came up and asked if we'd seen a golf ball. "Yep," I replied, "it came over the trees and landed right in the 'cup.'" Talk about being thrilled, he just couldn't believe it. He looked at the ball in the "cup" and then very excitedly turned around towards his fellow players and yelled, *"Fellas. . . . I got a nine!"*

One day, a bunch of us went deep sea fishing off the coast of Mexico. We decided to make a "pool" for the one who caught the first fish, so we each put up five dollars. All of a sudden, I got a marlin on the end of my line. Boy, what a fight that fish put up. During the struggle, I got excited and fell off the boat into the water. At this point, one of the men stuck his head over the side of the boat and yelled down to me, "If you're gonna dive for 'em . . . *No fair!"*

Horse racing may be the "Sport of Kings," but it's a business for "Touts." (In case you don't know what a "tout" is: he's one of those guys that hang around race tracks and try to influence your betting for their profit.) One day a "tout" grabbed me and said, "I got a horse for you that can't lose." I said, "What do you mean he *can't* lose?" His quick reply was, "The jockey's got halitosis and the horse'll win trying to get away from him!"

TICKET SELLER TO LOITERER: Gowan, Buddy, if you ain't gonna bet, get outa here.

LOITERER TO TICKET SELLER: Don't worry, wise guy, when I get ready to bet, I'm a big plunger.

TICKET SELLER TO LOITERER: Okay, big plunger, when the sink gets stopped up, we'll call you. *Now get outa here!*

One day, I went fishing with my brother Ted. In a short time, he caught the "limit" but I couldn't catch a darned thing. Next morning, I got up very early, took my brother's boat and equipment, and went out on the lake to try my luck. After over an hour without even a nibble, a fish stuck his head out of the water and said to me, "Hey . . . where's your brother?"

A few years ago, I was invited to entertain at one of the Dapper Dan Society dinners in Pittsburgh. One of the other speakers was the famous old baseball player, Honus Wagner. At this time, he was well in his eighties, but he still retained his great sense of humor. Seated in front of him as he spoke were some of the current baseball "greats." "You fellas make me laugh," Wagner said. "The least little ache or pain and you're out of the game." He continued, "When I played ball, we had tough men on the team. I'll never forget we had a guy who pitched sixteen winning games, then he lost one, and we dropped him!"

Two "sports" were playing golf for the first time, in the Catskill Mountains. Liebowitz shot the first hole in 320 strokes. Goldfarb shot the first hole in 419 strokes. As they walked towards the second tee, Goldfarb said, "You know something, Liebowitz, this golf is a very interesting game. How would you like to play for a nickel a hundred?"

How to Fish . . . and Why

Fishing is a gentleman's sport. As I once said to a woman who thought it was terrible for a big man to catch a poor little defenseless fish, "If the fish would have kept his mouth shut, he wouldn't have wound up with a hook in it." (This is irrelevant to the topic, but when I discuss fish, I discuss fish.)

There are many different kinds of fishing. I understand that on Catalina Island they fish in glass-bottom boats. That's so the fish can see how big the guy was they got away from. In Alaska, during the cold winter months, they fish with a watch and a hammer. They dig a hole in the ice and hold a watch over it . . . then when the fish come up to see what time it is, they hit 'em over the head with a hammer.

First, let us discuss the ordinary or humdrum type of fishing. For the novice, let me explain, that first of all one must have a fishing pole. This can easily be secured by cutting off a branch from your neighbor's favorite tree. Be careful not to kill any of the smaller branches on the tree as this sometimes makes your neighbor angry, and besides when they grow long enough, you can use them for poles next year.

Next is the tackle or line which must be of good quality. As a rule, the grocery store type is not strong enough to

hold a fish, but you will find a strong cord along the lower edge of his awning in front of the store. This may be cut with a pen-knife and wound into a ball. If you are careful, the awning should hold its position until an attempt is made to raise it. This sometimes causes it to fall into a pile on the ground. It is not advisable to offer the grocer suggestions at this time.

Next, one must decide as to the type of bait to be used. If you are going still-fishing, one must have worms. For bait, of course. Not personally! Although the ground type is preferred, there is also the apple worm. Somehow fish seem to be more inclined towards the large angle worm which you can also get on your neighbor's front lawn, after dark, with the aid of a flashlight. They are most commonly found under small flowers and plants, but it is not necessary to pull the plants up by the roots as the worm is usually close to the top. A common coffee can makes a good container for the bait, as it often comes in handy, after the worms are gone, for brewing excellent coffee. The mud does not alter the flavor; in fact it often restores its natural taste.

About half a can of worms is usually sufficient unless you are going to stay overnite. Then, some glowworms may be taken along to warm the atmosphere and make the dark night seem lighter.

For the fly type of fisherman, it is advisable to get three or four hundred ordinary houseflies, as they prove the best bait. These can be easily secured by letting your garbage stand around for three or four days. In the event of a fly shortage, wait until one lands in your soup, and then put a water glass over him while he is still in the soup. It is now but a matter of eating your soup from around the glass until the bowl is dry. Now you lift the glass and remove the fly whose wings are slightly green from the pea soup . . . that is . . . if you are having pea soup, and why not? Easy, isn't it?

Now you have tackle, pole, and bait. With a light lunch your wife can put up for you and a couple bottles of beer, you can borrow from your neighbor, you are ready to start. It is best to fish from a boat, if one can be secured. In this manner, you avoid hooking other people's lines and hats as one often does when fishing from the shore. If you do secure a boat, it is advisable to go out as far from shore as you can, because the fish out there are probably strangers and will not recognize you from last year. If you are fishing from shore, don't let crowds bother you. You can easily get a space by giving your nearest competitor a dirty look, or at worst, get a dirty look in return.

If one gets tired from sitting, it is generally the custom to walk around and ask other people if they caught anything and accidently knock over their bait can or trip over their pole. This usually brings forth a burst of laughter and makes friends for you very quickly.

When dusk falls and you are ready to return home, you may throw what remaining bait you have close to your neighbor's line, as this attracts the fish, and he will thank you for it.

I often wonder why other fishermen look at me and say, "The worm is on the wrong end of the pole."

Yes. Fishing is a gentleman's sport!

chapter eight

ANIMALS

(Or: The noblest of all dogs is the *hot dog*. It feeds
the hand that bites it.)
(Or: If everyone owned a horse, the country would be
more stabilized.)
(Or: A bird in the hand is not to be trusted.)

My uncle was always around wild animals: lions, tigers,
zebras, camels . . . he used to collect nickels on a merry-go-
round. My parents loved horses. They'd have given anything if I'd have been one. They were farmers. They raised
the biggest hog in the county. (Maybe I shouldn't be so
self-conscious.) I, myself, am very kind to animals. I give
half my money to the horses. (I bet on one last week that
came in so late he hadda walk on tiptoes to keep from
waking the other horses.) I love dogs too. And they love

me. When I walk down the street, they all run up and lick my fingers. (Maybe I should eat with a knife and fork.) I once had a dog that could pronounce his own name. His name was "Bow-wow." What a smart little animal! I once made a bet with a neighbor on whose dog was the smartest. We went down to the seashore and he threw a silver dollar into the water. His dog ran into the waves and brought back the silver dollar. I threw a silver dollar into the water and my dog brought back a herring and 30¢ change! Once, we had a fire and we couldn't find the dog. A short time later, he bounded out of the burning building carrying our fire insurance policy wrapped in a wet towel! We taught him how to bark and hold things in his mouth, but our house was robbed anyway. The dog couldn't bark because the burglars had him holding their flashlight. The name of the dog we have now, is *Pussycat*. Isn't that a terrible name for a dog? It's given him a complex. He's a real "Psycho," He doesn't know what he is. One day, when my son was about six years old, he had a friend over, and all day long we were saying, "Here, Pussycat . . . down, Pussycat . . . etc." Everytime we did, the kid would look at the dog in a very perplexed way. Finally, before he went home, he just couldn't contain himself any longer. Looking at Pussycat he exclaimed, "You know something . . . he looks just like a dog!"

I read in the paper that some scientist said we soon would be able to converse with animals. If that day ever comes, I'm gonna be the first one to walk up to a skunk and ask . . . *"What's the big idea?"*

I love animal stories.
Why don't you tell some?
I will.
And he did:

Two rabbits were being chased by a pack of wolves. Finally, one of the rabbits said to the other, "Why don't we stop for a minute and outnumber 'em?"

"How come your horse has got his feet in the feedbag?"
"Oh, he's just feeling his oats."

PET LOVERS: SAVE MONEY! Feed peanuts to your cat. Instead of milk, he'll drink water!

One day, a very-drunk Drunk was walking through the countryside. All of a sudden, he stopped short. There in front of him, coiled and in striking position, was a deadly rattlesnake. "Go ahead and strike," said the Drunk. "I was never better prepared!"

"How do porcupines make love?"
"Very cautiously."

Have you heard about the rich turtle who wore *people-neck* sweaters?

Two caterpillars were watching a butterfly soar through the air.
One caterpillar said to the other, "They'll never get *me* up in one of those things."

Then there's the story of the three fish: two herrings and one smelt.

"Do you know it takes five sheep to make one sweater?"
"I didn't even know they could knit."

To show you how you can fool the people; a man in Los Angeles is pinning badges on frankfurters and selling them for police dogs.

A man who bought a horse from a friend was warned that the horse had a bad habit of sitting on grapefruit. "I don't care if he's a grapefruit sitter," said the buyer. "I can break him of that." As they were galloping home, the horse saw some grapefruit several times and ran over and sat on it. His new owner just jabbed him with his spurs each time, and they traveled on. Suddenly, they came to a bridge, and the horse jumped off the bridge and sat down in the water. When they finally arrived home, the new owner, infuriated, telephoned the man from whom he had purchased the horse. "What kind of an animal did you sell me?" he shouted. His friend replied, "I told you he sits on grapefruit." "I expected that," was the answer, "but why did he jump off the bridge and sit in the water?" "Oops, I forgot to tell you," his friend said. *"He sits on fish, too!"*

"I think the elephants are leaving the zoo; I saw 'em
    pasting labels on their trunks."
"I wonder why they're leaving?"
"Maybe they're tired of working for peanuts."

Why doesn't somebody invent a flea powder that makes the fleas itch?

A salmon lays three thousand eggs a year and nobody remembers it on Mother's Day.

"I've got nine dogs."
"Did you buy 'em?"
"No, I whistle in my sleep."

A man who was perturbed at the bad picture he was getting on his TV decided to go up on the roof and check the antenna. He climbed up the ladder and as he poked his head over the edge of the roof he was surprised to see a parakeet sitting on the aerial screaming, *"What do you want? ? ?"* The man was so astonished that he apologetically said, "Excuse me, Sir, I thought you were a bird!"

I think my cat plays football. Last night he made two yards, tonight he's gonna make three.

The Papa Bear asked, "Whose been drinking my beer?"
The Mama Bear asked, "Whose been drinking my beer?"
The Baby Bear said, *"Hic!"*

Science is doing so much for animals:
They've crossed a carrier pigeon with a woodpecker so when he delivers the message he can knock on the door.
Crossed an ostrich with a bottle of Budweiser so they could get a glass of beer with its head in the ground.

They've crossed an octopus with a bale of hay and gotten a broom with eight handles.

And they've crossed a parrot with a boa constrictor. They don't know what they've got, but believe me, when it talks . . . *They listen!*

"What's the plural of hippopotamus?"
"Who wants more than one?"

I've heard a zebra described as a "Sport Model Jack-ass."

It wasn't because we had no cheese,
Nor on account of the cat.
The reason the mouse ran away from home, is
He found out his father was a rat!

"Daddy, how many kinds of milk are there?"
"Why do you want to know?"
"I'm drawing a picture of a cow and I don't know how many faucets to put on."

FARM TALK: One day on the farm, I was playing "follow the leader" with the animals. I did whatever they did. Everything went fine till some smart-aleck chicken laid an egg!

Our cow swallowed our midget radio. Now when we milk her we get three quarts of news flashes.

"That's a beautiful stuffed lion you've got there. Where did you get him?"

"In Africa, when I was on a hunting expedition with my uncle."

"What's he stuffed with?"

"My uncle."

A small family of skunks were being pursued by a wolf. They were cornered near a big tree at the edge of the forest. "Mama, what'll we do now," cried one of the baby skunks. The mother skunk softly answered, "Let us spray."

How to tell the difference between a male and female worm: The female worm doesn't signal when she turns.

A mother turkey was bawling out her children. "You bad kids," said the mother gobbler, "if your father could see you now, he'd turn over in his gravy!"

Three dogs, an English bull, a French poodle, and a Russian wolfhound were talking. The English bull and the French poodle agreed that they loved their respective countries and were content to stay there. The Russian wolfhound said, "I have the best of everything to eat and drink in Russia, but I sure would like to go to America." "How come?" the other two dogs asked. "Well," said the wolfhound, "I'd like to bark once in a while."

"My teeth hurt. It must be those animal crackers I was eating."

"But animal crackers are harmless little cookies."

"These were dog biscuits."

A famous violin virtuoso, tired of playing for people all over the world, decided he was going to play for animals only. Going into the deepest African jungle, he found a clearing, took out his violin, and started to play. The animals came from near and far and sat spellbound as the artist poured out lovely melodies. Suddenly a lion darted

out of the brush, pounced on the violinist, and ate him up! The other animals were furious. "What's the matter with you?" screamed one of the giant apes. "We were enthralled by this man's wonderful music, and you had to eat him up! Are you nuts or something ? ?" The lion put his paw up to his ear and asked, "Eh ? ?"

Last year the corn was so small, the sparrows had to kneel down to eat it.

My father was milking the cow when a cyclone hit and blew the cow three miles away! Left Paw holding the bag!

One day on the farm it was so windy that when we turned the hen the wrong way, she laid the same egg seven times!

"Do you believe that man comes from Monkeys?"
"I don't know. We're English. We come from Wales."

Once upon a time, there was a grasshopper and an ant. All during the summer, the ant worked very hard storing up food and supplies for the winter months. The grasshopper just hopped around, had a good time, and did no work. Came the cold, cold winter. The ant was comfortable in her little home with her well-stocked larder. The grasshopper was starving and miserable. Finally he asked the ant for help. She bawled him out for frittering away the whole summer, but felt sorry for him and took him in and gave him food and warmth. The moral of the story is: *if you're down and out, get yourself a rich old ant.*"

Two elephants were talking: "I don't care what people say," said one of them. "I can't remember a thing."

Two dogs were talking: One of them said, "Boy, what happened to me shouldn't happen to a man."

Two fleas were talking: "How're things?" asked one. "Fine," said the other, "I've saved up enough to buy my own dog."

Two flies were talking: "Is everything at home okay?" asked one. "No," said the other, "the baby is sick; I had to walk the ceiling with him all night."

Two cats were talking: "How come you always watch the tennis matches?" asked one. The other replied; "Because my brother is in the racket."

D'jer notice that every four years the elephants and donkeys have meetings to decide who're gonna make monkeys out of the people?

After hearing the roar of a high-powered rifle, the rancher ran out screaming at his hired hand: *"You fool . . . I said the horse was supposed to be shod!"*

"What makes you think your canary is nearsighted?"
"For two weeks, she's been trying to hatch a mothball."

A few years ago, I was booked into the Orpheum Theatre in Los Angeles, where I was "on the bill" with the Lone Ranger. I was very thrilled as he had always been one of my favorite stars. I rushed into the theatre very early on opening day as I couldn't wait to meet my idol. The Lone Ranger wasn't there yet, but his horse, Silver, was there. I had never seen such a magnificent animal, and I couldn't help saying it aloud. "What a beautiful horse,"

I said. The horse turned around, looked at me, and in flawless English remarked, "Think so?" Naturally, I was surprised to hear this horse talk in flawless English, especially inasmuch as he was an "Arabian Steed." He didn't even have a trace of an accent. We got to talking and found out we had some mutual friends at Grossinger's Hotel. (I discovered later that the horse's real name was Silver*stein*.) "Just off the record," I asked the horse, "how is this working for the Lone Ranger?" The horse looked at me, whinnied a second, and remarked, "Stinks." I was dumbfounded. "The Lone Ranger, big man," snorted Silver, "I do all the work and he takes bows. When it comes to chasing cattle rustlers, I'm doing the running . . . when you see pictures of him sitting in my saddle, overlooking the valley . . . who gets him up there? Me! You're looking at a horse that works like a dog! Do you know why he wears that mask? He knows if I ever recognize him away from work, I'll kick his teeth in!" "Wow," I said, "I had no idea he was such a slave driver!" At that moment the horse looked around and said to me, "Shhhh." "What's the matter?" I inquired. "Here comes the Lone Ranger now," he replied. *"If he knows I can talk he'll have me yelling 'Hi Yo Silver. ! ! ' "*

A drunk who had gotten lost in the frozen wastes of the Swiss Alps suddenly saw a big St. Bernard dog coming towards him, with a small barrel of brandy hanging from his collar. "At last," said the boozer, "here comes Man's best friend, attached to a dog!"

Did you hear about the nearsighted snake who fell in
love with a piece of rope?

I love to ride horseback. The other day, I went to a place called The Gardenia Livery Stables, (and don't let the name fool you). They gave me a horse that was so sway-backed, they had to put high heels on his horseshoes to keep his stomach from dragging. Besides that, the stirrups on his saddle were too long and his hind legs kept getting caught in 'em. I finally said to the horse, "Look if you're gonna get on and ride, I'll get off and walk." Luckily he had four legs, but they were all in single file. I rode about a block from the stables and the horse fell down, so I went back and got another horse. I rode about two blocks and *he* fell down. This happened about six times. Finally, I went back to the stable master and told him that I had rented six horses and each one had fallen down. "Don't get mad," he told me. "Go 'way in the back of the stable and you'll see about a hundred horses lined up there. Take anyone you want, but don't take the one in the middle or they'll *all* fall down!"

You Can't Milk a Cow with a Monkey Wrench.

A family of sparrows was flying south for the winter. Arriving in Memphis, the mother sparrow was alarmed to notice that one of her brood was missing. After waiting for several worried hours, the lost baby sparrow showed up. "Where have you been?" asked Mama Sparrow. "Well," said the fledgling, "it was such a nice day, I thought I'd walk."

chapter nine

POEMS, LIMERICKS, AND ALL
THAT KINDA JAZZ

(Or: Shelley and I were Keats together.)
(Or: He sat on the Brooklyn Bridge dangling his feet
in the water . . . Longfellow.)

I've always been nutty about poetry. Especially nutty
poetry. When I was a kid, I used to write poetry on the
walls of the little boys' room. Some of it is still there . . .
which is probably the reason they have a plaque on the
desk where I used to sit, which reads, "Condemned by
the Board of Health." We had a big, fat English teacher
who asked us to write a poem dedicated to her. Her name

was Miss Crass. Needless to say my rhyme got me ex-pelled. I got most of my poetry-writing experience when I spent four years putting up highway signs for Burma Shave. I think it was Voltaire who said, "Poetry is like a taxicab . . . it must have good meter." I really don't know whether or not it was Voltaire who said that, but *I* ain't gonna take the blame. All of which has nothing to do with the following:

> Mary had a little lamb
> So nice, so fat, so round,
> She walked him by a butcher shop,
> Oops, 69¢ a pound!

Darling little rabbit with your eyes of pink,
Laugh, be gay, have fun today, tomorrow you may be a
  mink.

I've got an aunt named Minnie,
Weighs three hundred and sixty-four.
When she sits on a chair, there's so much of her there,
Most of her sits on the floor.

> Rub-a-dub-dub
> Three men in a tub
> Do you think that's sanitary?

Some folks wanna be in the ballet and dance upon their
  toes,
I'd rather be an elephant and squirt water through my
  nose.

My mother-in-law has passed away,
For her my heart doth yearn,
I know she's with the angels now
'Cause she was too tough to burn.

A Poor Old Man's Prayer

I'm much too old for bicycles, or wagons, or for skates,
But dear Lord won't you please send me some brand new
  dental plates?
It ain't my looks that worry me 'cause I'm beyond conceit,
And I can "gum" my gravy, while others bite their meat.
But I gotta have them dental plates, oh dear Lord, I
  beseech,
I need 'em 'specially on the days I go out to the beach,
'Cause the thing that makes me so durned mad I just stand
  there and bristle
Is . . . all them beautiful babes go by and I can't even
  whistle!

We met on a Pullman sleeper,
I shall never forget the place.
I was coming down from an upper berth,
And I stepped right on her face.

I like your style,
I like your smile,
I like your walk,
I like your talk,
But *I don't like you!*

You'll never see this come to pass,
A backseat driver out of gas.

STUDENT'S POEM

I love to do my English, it makes me feel so good.
I love to do exactly as my teacher thinks I should.
I love my school so very much, I never ditch a day,
I even love the men in white who are taking me away.

Curious fly
Vinegar jug
Slippery edge
Pickled bug.

Don't worry if your job is small and your rewards are few.
Remember that the mighty oak was once a nut like you.

Little Jack Horner
Sat in the corner
B. O.

Thirty days has September
And my Uncle Ben . . . for speeding.

A burglar broke into our house
This morning at half past three,
If you're wondering if he got anything,
He did,
My wife thought it was me.

Song of Summer

Little bankroll, ere we part,
Let me press you to my heart,
All the year I've clung to you,
I've been faithful, you've been true,
Little bankroll in a day,
You and I will start away
To a good vacation spot,
I'll come back, but you will not.

There was a little girl, and she had a little curl,
Right in the middle of her forehead,
And when she was good, she was very very good,
And when she was bad . . . wow, did she become popular!

She stood on the bridge at midnight,
It was so cold, it made her shiver,
She gave a cough,
And her hat blew off,
And the wind blew up the river!

If things go bad, old Buddy,
And your mind is in a fog,
Remember, if you need a friend,
Go out and buy a dog.

Garry Moore gave me this one:

It's easy to grin when your ship comes in,
And life is a happy lot,
But the guy who's worth-while
Is the guy who can smile,
When his shorts creep up in a knot.

To My Wife

My wife has such a lovely voice,
As mellow as can be,
But she does pick the darndest times
To start talking to me.

My wife has such a lovely voice,
With soft tones underneath,
But why does she ask me questions,
When I'm in the middle of brushing my teeth?

You may have seen the leaning tower of Pisa,
You may have seen the Taj Mahal, the sacred surging
    Ganges, the Lamaseries in Tibet,
But until you've eaten lobster and ice cream before going
    to bed,
Boy . . . you ain't seen nothin' yet!

To market, to market, to buy a fat pig,
Pork chops are small, prices are big,
Home again, home again, can't afford that,
Never mind, butcher, I'll just eat the cat.

I love to sing the high notes,
I sing 'em with all my might,
I'd like to sing much higher,
But my underwear's too tight.

Tobacco is a filthy weed,
I like it.
It satisfies no normal need,
I like it.
It makes you fat; it makes you lean,
It keeps your wits from being keen,
Its the worst darned stuff I've ever seen,
I like it.

We've got a guy lives on our block,
What an absent-minded "gink,"
He always kisses the dishes good night,
Then throws his wife in the sink.

My brother has a square stomach,
It may sound strange, but it's true,
He doesn't only eat all his cereal,
He eats the boxes too.

I like the Stage Delicatessen,
I think their food is best,
Because at the Stage Delicatessen,
They make gravy to match your vest.

I once knew a very conceited girl,
And all men she did hate,
"Plenty of fish in the sea," she said,
But she finally ran out of bait.

Jack be nimble,
Jack be quick,
Jack jump over the candlestick,
Big deal!

When children are naughty and cranky,
Don't put o'er your knee and spanky,
Or without dinner, don't send 'em to bed,
Just grab a crowbar and hit 'em in the head!

If you have a terrible cold in your head,
And it's making you a wreck,
You can keep it from going down into your chest
By tying a knot in your neck.

The guy next door to me
I think has "flipped his noodle,"
He ties his dog to the end of a stick
And mops up the floor with his poodle.

chapter ten

LEFTOVERS

(Or: They threw me out of Texas because I forgot
the Alamo.)
(Or: I'll never forget the girl to whom I was once
engaged . . . because I'm still paying for the engagement
ring.)

I've always been very absent-minded. For instance,
when our daughter was born, and the nurse said, "Con-
gratulations, your wife just had a baby girl," I asked who
the lucky father was. This morning, when I cut my finger,
I forgot to bleed. Very often I will throw my clothes on the
bed and lie down in the closet. One morning, at breakfast, I
poured the syrup down my back, scratched my pancakes,

and then handed the waiter a knife and fork and said, "Keep the change." Well, I've had the same kind of trouble with this book. Each time, a few days after I would turn in a chapter to the publishers, I would say to myself, "Listen, Stupid. (I always call myself "Listen.") Isn't there something you forgot to include?" And each time, I was right. I kept finding a bunch of stuff lying around in the back of my head, so I've sneezed, cleared my head, and dumped it all into this last chapter. Hence, "Leftovers." (They say that leftovers are much better when they're cold. Well, after looking over the following, I don't think it's so hot.)

"Doctor, I'm suffering from amnesia."
"How long have you had it?"
"Had what?"

An old "sourdough" was lost in the Alaskan wilderness. He hadn't eaten in several days, and in a last desperate effort to stave off starvation, he killed his faithful dog, Rover, cooked him, and ate him. As he ate the meat off each bone, he piled the bones into a neat pile. Suddenly he gazed at the bones, and tears came to his eyes as he said to himself, "Gee, Rover would have loved those bones."

An old lady, standing in front of a peanut stand was listening to the "peanut whistle" through an old-fashioned ear trumpet. Finally she said to the peanut man, "I wouldn't give you a nickel for that music. You can't tell what the tune is, and it smells like something's burning!"

Indians used to broadcast messages by holding a wet blanket over the fire. Today we have TV and you can see the wet-blanket, in person.

How to make a small room look larger: Use thin wallpaper.

SOMETHING BADLY NEEDED DEPT.:
A spot remover that removes the spots left by other spot removers.

A raisin is a worried grape.

Why waste your life looking for that pot of gold at the end of the rainbow, when you can put a penny in a scale and get a fortune.

A man walked into a medical center and the nurse asked him, "Which doctor do you wish to see?" The man replied, "I don't wanna see no witch doctor, I wanna see a regular one!"

Ole Tom Jones was known as a very shrewd but philanthropic man. One day, a church member approached him for a donation. "What's it for?" asked Tom. "Well," replied the lady, "we want to get a big, new bell for the church tower, so when it rings, it will be loud enough for everyone in town to hear it, and we will get new members for the congregation." Ole Tom asked her, "Didn't I give you a couple-hundred dollars last year to put a new furnace in the basement of the church?" "You certainly did," she replied. "Well," said Tom, "then you don't need no new bell. Just run a steampipe up from the furnace to the roof, put a whistle on it, and folks'll hear ya for miles . . ! !"

ABOUT MY LAUNDRY

My laundryman phoned today; he was very upset. He forgot to tear one of my collars. What a mean guy! He knew I had a cold so he's been starching my handkerchiefs. He doesn't even wash my shirts, he just sharpens the collars. He has no sense of humor. I once sent him a bag of buttons with a note saying, "Just for a change, sew on a few." The whole Union came to see me! I used to have a habit of writing jokes down on the cuff of my sleeves. Now my laundryman has his own TV show! (All clean material.)

A sailor had a pair of bloomers tattooed on his chest because he always wanted a chest with drawers.

SAD STORY: She was a fine musician. All her life she played the harp. When she died, she didn't go to heaven. What a waste!

I had a beautiful suit made of awning material. There was only one thing wrong with it; everytime the sun went down, the pants roll'd up!

"I hear that in South America they're making dresses out of glass."

"So long, I'm going to South America."

"Are you a glass blower?"

"No, I'm a window washer!"

One advantage in being bald is, when company comes in unexpectedly, all you have to do is straighten your tie.

Ladies: When you walk into a room, do the men holler and scream . . . and then run and hide? Well, *stay outa locker rooms!!*

I know a guy, who got so hepped up on reincarnation, he went to his attorney, changed his will, and left everything to himself!

An old man, who lay dying, dictated his last will to his lawyer. "To my son," he said, "I leave $100,000, and to his children, I leave $3000 each." The lawyer looked at him in astonishment. "You must be crazy," he said. "Why your whole estate isn't worth over $5000! Where will they get the money?" The old man raised himself from his pillow and screamed, "Let 'em go out and work for it, like I did!!"

Did you hear about the girl who was seriously hurt while taking a milk bath? The cow slipped on a piece of soap and fell on her head!

Since the President found out how much money they made at the Hialeah Race Track last year, he wants to take out Congress and put in horses!

The warden, making his rounds at the asylum, noticed one of the inmates sitting on a small stool holding a fishing pole. He had the end of the line dangling in the wash basin. Trying to be kind, the warden inquired, "Catching anything?" "Are you nuts?" was the reply. "In a wash basin??"

Cow: Moo. . . .
Rich Cow: Lotsa Moo.

I was in a house the other day where the furniture was so old it was all paid for.

Two space men from the moon, landed on the Earth and seeing all the television aerials on the rooftops, one nudged the other and said, "Hey, look . . . *dames!*"

Advertisement: Gigengack's Breakfast Food. The break-fast food that makes dinner a pleasure . . . 50% iron, 20%

zinc and 30% lead. Doesn't snap, crack, or pop . . . just lays in your stomach and goes, *clang! clang!*

I know a guy who runs a combination pawnshop and butcher shop. He has three meatballs hanging over the door!

This bump on my head is called a "curiosity bump." I was looking to see if the elevator was coming up and it was coming down.

Save your money. Some day it may be worth something!

I didn't know she wore a false upper plate till it came out in the conversation.

The reason it takes women so much longer to dress is because they have to slow down on the curves.

Epitaph on the tombstone of a hypochondriac: *"See . . . I told you I was sick."*

A bachelor, left in charge of his baby nephew, suddenly faced that well-known problem. Frantically, he called a friend who was, luckily, a father. The bachelor was coached thusly: "Place the diaper in the position of a baseball diamond, with you at bat. Fold second base over home plate. Place nephew on pitcher's mound, then pin first base and third base at home plate!"

This is supposed to be a true story. After listening to a

long-winded speech by a certain congressman, he was introduced to the public official. The congressman said, "So you're Thomas Edison, the man who invented the talking machine, eh?" "No," replied Edison, "God invented the talking machine . . . I just invented one that could be turned off."

FOR SALE: Lighthouse. Suitable for tall, thin man who likes sea gulls.

Some people think the only way to make both ends meet is by collapsing in the middle.

They say that if your hand itches . . . you're gonna get it. I guess if your head itches . . . you've got it!

Definition of a true musician: One who, when he hears a lady singing in the bathtub, he puts his *ear* to the keyhole.

I look out through my window and I see the distant shore, I look out through my window . . . I can't see a darned thing through my door.

SONG TITLE: My girl to me is a perfect stranger, since she caught her face in the record changer.

I know a guy who hasn't got an enemy in the world, but all his friends hate him.

I always use the dial phone,
With me it never fails,

I never get my number,
But it manicures my nails.

STUBBORN CITIZEN: I wouldn't vote for you if you were
St. Peter himself!
LOCAL POLITICIAN: If I was St. Peter, you wouldn't be
in my precinct!

Two new members of a nudist colony were discussing
another member who had an exceptionally long beard.
They finally decided to ask him about it. "Say, Pop, how
come we are all completely nude, and you have a long
beard that covers you well below the knees?" The old man
replied, "Well, boys . . . somebody has to go for the coffee!"

Life is an everlasting struggle to keep money coming
in and hair and teeth from coming out!

In a recent interview, some evangelist said there are
seven hundred and eighty-five sins. He is now besieged
by requests for the list, mostly from people who think
they're missing something.

They sure do everything big down in Texas. In Dallas,
one day, I saw a flea walking down the street with six
dogs on him.

"I've been playing the piano on and off, for years."
"On and off??"
"Yeah . . . slippery stool."

The mortuaries in Florida are so beautiful, if you're
alive, you feel like you're missing something.

A small wholesaler collected many past-due accounts through the use of the following statement:

"If you will refer to the date of our original invoice you will note that we have done more for you than your own mother. We have carried you for fourteen months!"

A lady who was driving behind a truck loaded with newspapers saw a bale of the papers fall from the swiftly moving vehicle. The lady, always ready to be helpful, stopped and put the load into the back seat of her own car. Continuing on, she noticed several other bundles of the papers on the road and retrieved these too. Farther up the road, she came upon the truck, parked outside of a diner. She went in and proudly told the truck driver what she had done. "You got my papers in your car?" he exploded. "For gosh sakes, lady. . . . *I was delivering 'em!!*"

"Do you think the Senator put enough fire into his speech?"

"I don't think he put enough of his speech into the fire."

Takes two to make a marriage. A single girl and an anxious mother.

Next year, they're gonna have a football team made up of mother-in-laws. Boy, what interference!

If speed was everything, rabbits would rule the world, and we'd all be on the $1.50 plate dinner.

SIGN IN BAKERY WINDOW: Cakes . . . 66¢. Upside down cakes . . . 99¢.

A masked man walked up to the cashier in a theatre ticket-window. "Stick 'em up," he said. "The picture is lousy, gimmie back everybody's money!"

A lot of people get credit for being well behaved because they don't have the money to do otherwise.

I know a guy who's been dispossessed so many times, he has drapes to match the sidewalk.

A psychiatrist received a card from a patient who was on vacation. It read: *Having a wonderful time . . . why?*

"My uncle makes a lot of money in gambling joints."
"How?"
"When cops raid the joint, he grabs all the money off the tables and runs and hides."
"What if the cops don't show up?"
"He calls 'em."

We come from a very sentimental family. My uncle died while playing a pinball machine, so we *tilted* his tombstone.

I was seated in a barber shop the other afternoon, when some man ran in, handed the barber his toupee and said, "Gimmie a haircut and a shampoo; I'll be back in a half hour."

SIGN ON APARTMENT: *Saxophone for Sale.*
SIGN ON NEXT APARTMENT: *Hooray!*

"Who is that lovely girl sitting over there, with the string of pearls around her neck?"
"I don't know."
"And I wonder who that man is, that's with her."
"Probably the oyster the pearls came from."

My barber once cut me up pretty nicely. I had so many slashes in my face, I had to drink water to see if my mouth leaked. After he got through shaving me, he asked, "Would you like me to wrap your head in a hot towel?"
"No," I replied, "I'll just carry it home under my arm!"

"Have you ever been in Albuquerque?"
"I dunno. I'll have to go home and look through my towels."

"My doctor said I could cure my cold by drinking a glass of orange juice after a hot bath."

133

"Did you drink the orange juice?"
"I haven't finished drinking the hot bath yet."

The Treasury department is getting very generous. After you pay your taxes, they give you a mirror so you can go home and watch yourself starve to death.

If conditions get any worse you won't have to go to the poorhouse. Stay home. Your house is as good as theirs.

"This dress is tighter than my skin."
"Impossible."
"Oh yeah? Well I can sit down in my skin, but I'll be darn if I can sit down in this dress."

A large steamship, fogbound, suddenly stopped in the middle of the ocean. One of the lady passengers rushed up to the captain and asked, "Why are we stopped?" The captain replied that it was impossible to proceed as they were entirely surrounded by fog. The woman looked directly overhead, where there was a small clearing in the sky, pointed to the stars and said, "Look, Captain, it's clear up there." The captain replied, "Lady, unless the boiler explodes, we aren't going that way."

Advertisement: Try our new cold cream. It takes the wrinkles out of prunes. It won't do anything for your face, but you'll have the smoothest prunes in town.

What really started all the trouble in the Garden of Eden is: Eve put Adam's Sunday suit in the salad!

My pal, conductor-composer Milton Delugg, loves stories of the old west. He tells about the cowboy who was going to be burned at the stake by the Indians. After the red men had him securely tied, the chief walked over to the cowboy and handed him a blanket. "What's this for?" asked the cowboy. The chief replied, "To keep you warm till we start the fire."

"How did you get up in that oak tree?"
"When I was a kid, I sat on an acorn."

On his tenth anniversary as a band leader, a famous maestro who had played some two thousand dance jobs was asked what he had the most requests for. His quick reply was, "Directions to the men's room."

Former child-star Rosemarie, who is now one of Show Biz's top singing comediennes, loves "drunk" stories. One of her favorites is about the boozer who had been out on a "bender" that must have been "written by Eugene O'Neill." (It ran so long.) Coming out of a drunken haze, he suddenly remembered he had a wife and family. Phoning his wife at 5 a.m., he was trying to be nonchalant. "Hello, honey," he said, "whatcha got for dinner tonight?" Her disgusted answer was, "Oh, rats." His quick reply was, "Only cook half, I ain't coming home." "You'd better come home," she told him, "or, I'll trace this call, find you, and fracture your skull!" "All right," he said, "don't get mad, I'm coming right home. Get the kids off the street, I'm driving!" Naturally, after being "loaded" for so many months, he didn't know where his car was, so he got on a local suburban train and started home. Realizing he looked pretty sloppy with about a two weeks' growth of beard, he borrowed a razor, shaving cream, and a mirror and went into the men's room. He hung the mirror on the wall, lathered up, and just as he was about to start shaving, he dropped the razor. As he bent down to pick it up, the train lurched, and the mirror fell off of the wall. Not realizing this, he stood up and stared at the blank wall, "Oh my God," he exclaimed, *"I cut my head off!!"*

A farmer who had been on a trip to Honolulu was back home and explaining to his neighbor how the "Hula" is done. "They put a crop of hay in front and a crop of hay in back and just rotate their crops."

SOCIETY NOTE: When you're invited to tea, just make conversation and pass the bag.

I know a guy who's so rich he goes to drive-in movies in a taxi.

Washington, D. C. Where the skeletons in the closets are ashamed of the people who live in the houses.

Nothing is ever all wrong. Even a clock that stops is right twice a day.

NEVER SATISFIED DEPT.: Winter is the season of the year when we try to keep the house as hot as it was in the summer, when we kept complaining about the heat.

Dear Cooking Expert: I listened to your cake recipe over the radio and baked a cake for my husband, according to your directions. He ate the cake and just sat there and smiled. Come over any day, *he's still sitting there, smiling.*

Of the many stories I often tell on "personal appearances," my wife's favorite is the one about the girl who was driving along the highway about seventy miles an hour, when she noticed a speed cop following her, so she drove faster. Pretty soon, there were two speed cops following her, and in short order, five more. Suddenly coming to a gas station, she pulled in, stopped, jumped out of her car and ran into the ladies' room. Coming out, about five minutes later, here were the seven policemen, draped over their motorcycles, just waiting for her. She gave them a sweet smile and said, "Say, I'll bet you boys didn't think I was gonna make it!"

A Boston lady was expressing her indignation at the indecent words she saw scribbled on some walls and sidewalks of the city. "What will outsiders think of us?" she cried. "Why some of the words aren't even spelled correctly!"

Russian weather report: Tomorrow sunny. That's an order!

A chestnut is a guy who's nuts about chests.

A notorious bookmaker died and left a widow and five policemen without means of support.

Conductor, *Conductor! Lemme off this train!* I thought it was a lunch wagon.

"Pull up a chair and sit down."
"I just came from the livery stable."
"Oh, well pull up a window and sit down."

A couple of hoboes came to a backdoor and asked the lady of the house for some food. She said to them, "See that big rug hanging out there on the line? Well, beat the dirt out of that rug, and I'll give you both a nice lunch." They each got a large bat and started beating the rug. A short time later, the lady glanced out of the window and was surprised to see one of the bums jumping in the air, doing somersaults and back flips. She went out and said to the other man, "I didn't know your partner was an acrobat." He replied, "Neither did I, till I hit him in the shins with this bat!"

People who live in glass houses might as well answer the doorbell.

"I crossed a horse with a fish."
"How?"
"I put a fin on a horse's nose."

A bookie who had lost his mind and was sent to an asylum kept right on booking horses. The inmates, having no money to bet with, used rocks and pebbles. One day, one of them walked up to the bookie, carrying a large boulder. He laid it on the table and said, "Bet this on

Lady Lucille in the fifth." Two of the other inmates, seeing the large boulder being bet, said, "Hmmmm . . . he must know something."

"How'd you get that bump on your head?"
"I sent away for some hair tonic and they sent me bust developer by mistake."

I like chocolate cake. It doesn't show the dirt.

Short History Quiz

Q: What happened in 1776?
A: What a party! I was in 1777 across the hall!
Q. How come George Washington stood up when they cross'd the Delaware?
A: He knew if he sat down, somebody'd hand him an oar.
Q: Why did Napoleon wear his hat sideways?
A: Military strategy. He didn't want the enemy to know which way he was going!

A friend of mine is crazy about limburger cheese, you know, the imported kind that's so strong it comes over on its own strength. He was making a trip out to St. Louis, and he put a nice big "cake" of the very strong cheese into his valise. When he arrived at the hotel in St. Louis, the odor was so powerful, it almost blew the lid off of the grip. His wife said, "For heaven's sakes, get rid of that stuff, it smells awful!" He started looking around for a place to throw it, that would be inconspicuous and he finally found a potted plant on the window ledge. He took the plant out of the pot, put the cheese in it, and replaced the plant. Six weeks later, when he was back in New York, he received a telegram from the manager of the hotel, which read: *"We give up . . . where is it??"*

Which reminds me of the story about the man who was asked if he put very strong cheese in the mousetrap. His reply was, "All I know is, it's the first time I've ever seen mice *back* into a trap."

"My feet hurt. I guess I've been biting my nails again."

PECULIAR JOBS: The man who eats moth balls all winter and in the summer time, he has a nice job breathing on overcoats.

I know a girl who is so dumb, she once followed a water sprinkler down the street for six blocks to tell the man his wagon was leaking.

Some doctors should be more careful. One of them,

who didn't know my uncle was a cement mixer, told him he should lose himself in his work. My uncle is now a left turn on route 66!

There is definitely no human life on the planet, Mars. They have never asked the United States for a loan.

There seems to be plenty of money in the country, but everyone owes it to everyone else.

He's the kind of fellow who knows a lot; he just can't think of it.

Mohammed says: "Confucius talk too much."

A lot of suburban dwellers have discovered that trees grow on money.

A cannibal is a man who goes into a restaurant and orders the waiter.

Sign in Tailor Shop: We are sure our suits last twenty-five years. We have been in business twenty-five years, and nobody has ever come back for a second suit.

Home cooking is something a fella's mother gives him, so that by the time he gets married, he can't eat anything.

A college education is something that enables you to work for someone who hasn't any education at all.

We don't know where our next meal is coming from. Our cook is cockeyed.

Money may not buy happiness, but with it, you can be miserable in comfort.

WANTED: Job as secretary. No bad habits . . . willing to learn.

WANTED: Job as elevator operator. No experience. Will start in low building.

"What's the difference between vegetable soup and hash?" "They're both the same . . . only vegetable soup's looser."

A friend of mine claims he lost a fortune over night. He went to bed feeling like a million and woke up feeling like two cents.

The laziest man I ever heard of lived down near my cousin's farm. One day, my cousin drove by the man's farm and noticed his barn was on fire. "Your barn's burning down!" my cousin screamed at him. "I know it," the lazy one replied. "I'm sittin' here prayin' for rain."

My uncle was so bow-legged that my aunt hung him over the door for good luck.

Two good friends passed away on the same day. One went to Heaven and the other one went to Hell. One day, the man in Heaven telephoned his friend down below:

"How're things down there?" he inquired. His friend replied, "Great . . . Man . . . this is a ball! They give you a little red suit . . . a hot poker . . . plenty of booze and broads . . . parties all the time. . . . I never had it so good. How're things with you?" His friend from Heaven replied, "I never worked so hard. Every day I have to deliver milk to the Milky Way . . . polish up the stars . . . push the clouds around . . . Man . . . I'm beat." His friend in the "Hot Place" asked, "How come you got so much work?" His angel-friend replied, " 'Cause I'm the only one up here!"

A girl walked into a drugstore and told the druggist she would like to buy some rat poison. "Would you like to take it with you?" the druggist asked. Annoyed at the silly question, the girl replied, "No, I'll send the rats in after it!"

"What is your nationality?"
"I don't know, I was born at sea."
"Then you're the nationality of your mother."
"But I was traveling with my aunt at the time."

I know a guy who is such a low-brow that when he gets a headache, he puts the aspirin in his shoes.

ADVERTISEMENT: Robinson Crusoe Loan Company. Do you need money over the weekend? See our man Friday.

LANDLORD: You're six months behind in your rent. I'll give you three more days to pay up. Remember . . . just three more days.
SCOTCHMAN: All rrrright, I'll take Christmas, Fourth of July, and New Year's!

Two stuttering blacksmiths were working together. One of them had just taken the red hot horse shoe out of the fire and placed it on the anvil. He said to his partner, "G-g-g-g-go ahead and hi-hi-hi-hit it." His partner asked, "Wh-wh-wh-wh-where should I hi-hi-hi-hi-hit it?" "Oh, h-h-h-hell," replied the first blacksmith, "now I'll have to h-h-h-h-heat it all over again!"

ETC. ETC. ETC. ETC. ETC.

If you like this book, don't loan it to your friends. Let 'em go out and buy one. (The money goes to a good cause, the *Send-the-Amsterdams-to-Europe-for-the-Summer* fund.) If you don't like it, *keep your big mouth shut.* (Your friends may buy it anyway. Let 'em make their own mistakes.) Keep a laugh in your heart. Keep well and happy. This is all for now.

—MOREY

CPSIA information can be obtained
at www.ICGtesting.com
Printed in the USA
LVHW012034190723
752844LV00012B/596